Walking
with the
Holy Spirit

Thirty Days of
Spiritual Discovery

Denzil R. Miller

Unless otherwise noted, Scripture quotations are from the HOLY BIBLE, NEW INTERNATIONAL VERSION®. NIV®. Copyright © 1973, 1978, 1984 by International Bible Society. Used by permission of Zondervan.

Biblical quotations marked KJV are taken from the KING JAMES VERSION (KJV): KING JAMES VERSION, public domain.

Biblical quotations marked NASB are taken from the NEW AMERICAN STANDARD BIBLE® Copyright © 1960, 1962, 1963, 1968, 1971, 1972, 1973, 1975, 1977, 1995 by The Lockman Foundation. Used by permission.

Biblical quotations marked ESV are taken from the HOLY BIBLE, ENGLISH STANDARD VERSION (ESV): Scriptures taken from THE HOLY BIBLE, ENGLISH STANDARD VERSION® Copyright © 2001 by Crossway, a publishing ministry of Good News Publishers. Used by permission.

Biblical quotations marked TLB are taken from the LIVING BIBLE copyright© 1971. Used by permission of Tyndale House Publishers, Inc., All rights reserved.

Biblical Quotations marked NLT are taken from the HOLY BIBLE, NEW LIVING TRANSLATION Copyright © 1996, 2004, 2007 by Tyndale House Foundation. Used by permission of Tyndale House Publishers

Miller, Denzil R., 1946—
www.DenzilRMiller.com
Walking with the Holy Spirit: Thirty Days of Spiritual Discovery.
/ Denzil R. Miller.

1. Biblical studies   2. Holy Spirit   3. Pneumatology—Pentecostal
4. Missions—Strategy   5. Theology—Pastoral

ISBN: 978-0-9971750-4-2

PneumaLife Publications
3766 N. Delaware Ave.
Springfield, MO 65803
2017

Printed in the United States of America

Contents

Part 5: The Baptism in the Holy Spirit

Part 6: The Holy Spirit Helps Us

Part 7: Living and Ministering in the Holy Spirit

Introduction

In May of 2015, the *Calgary Sun* of Calgary, Ontario, Canada, ran an article entitled, "After 23-Year Search, Ontario Man Meets Brother He Never Knew." The article describes how 68-year-old Dave Smith discovered he had an elder brother while rummaging through papers left behind by his recently deceased mother. The documents revealed that his mother had given up his brother for adoption before Smith was born. Smith then began a search that would last 23 years. He finally located his brother living in Edinberg, Scotland. The brothers have now been united. Smith testified, "It was really amazing for me. It's like we've known each other all our lives."

Many Christians today are much like Dave Smith. They have a heavenly "Elder Brother" whom they've never really gotten acquainted with—the Holy Spirit. Someone once referred to the Holy Spirit as "the God we hardly know." Another has called Him "the ignored member of the Holy Trinity." I once listened to an evangelical scholar say, "We describe ourselves as being 'Trinitarians'; however, in actual practice we are really 'Binitarians.' The Father we know, and the Son we know, but we really don't know the Holy Spirit."

Frances Chan concurs. In his book, *Forgotten God,* he says, "From my perspective, the Holy Spirit is tragically neglected and, for all practical purposes, forgotten" in many churches today. He continues, "There is a big gap between what we read in Scripture about the Holy Spirit and how most believers and churches operate today." Chan describes this widespread ignorance of the Spirit as a "prolific disease in the church today." While Chan is talking about non-Pentecostal Evangelicalism, his indictment could sadly apply to many, if not most, Pentecostal churches today.

During the past 25 years, my wife Sandy and I have served as Assemblies of God missionaries to Africa. We lead a ministry called the Acts in Africa Initiative. The ministry aims at "mobilizing the African church for Spirit-empowered mission." In recent years, our AIA team has conducted more than 50 "Acts 1:8 Conferences" in 38 countries in Sub-Saharan Africa and the Indian Ocean Basin. In these missions mobilization conferences, we have marveled at how our African brothers and sisters have embraced the empowering work of the Holy Spirit and how their lives and ministries have been dramatically transformed as a result.

When in America, we often minister in churches, soliciting financial and prayer support. I frequently preach on the Holy Spirit and His work in missions. It is not unusual to have someone come up to me afterward, and say, "Your message today is the first message I've heard on the Holy Spirit in years. In our church we hardly ever hear about the Holy Spirit." (Just to be clear, this happens in so-called "Pentecostal" churches.) Because of this shameful neglect of the Spirit, there exists in the church a widespread ignorance concerning His nature and work.

This book seeks to address, a least in part, this troubling state of affairs. In it, I will lead you on a journey of spiritual discovery. During the next 30 days, we will rediscover who the Holy Spirit is and how we may know Him better. We will further discover how He will empower us and enable us to do our part in fulfilling God's mission in the earth.

Someone may ask, "Can one really have a loving relationship with the Holy Spirit?" When you think about it, this is a strange question. After all, the Holy Spirit is the One who pours God's love into our hearts (Rom. 5:5). He is the "Third Person of the Trinity." Just as the Father is God, and the Son is God, the Holy Spirit is God. And, as God, the Holy Spirit is a divine Person. And since He is a Person, then we can know Him and live in relationship with Him.

In writing to the Christians in Philippi, Paul spoke of the "fellowship of the Spirit" (Phil. 2:1). The Greek word here translated "fellowship" is *koinonia*. It signifies a deep, intimate relationship with another person. Thus, when Paul speaks of fellowship with the Holy Spirit, he is describing a loving, living relationship that we may have with Him.

The night before Jesus was crucified, He met with His disciples in an upper room. He told them that the day was coming when they would enjoy the same relationship with the Holy Spirit that they now had with Him. Jesus began by telling them that He was about to leave them. Then He promised, "I will not leave you as orphans. I will come to you" (John 14:18, ESV). This was a promise of the Holy Spirit, whom Jesus said He would send in His place. "I will ask the Father," He said, "and he will give you another Helper, to be with you forever, even the Spirit of truth, whom the world cannot receive, because it neither sees him nor knows him. You know him, for he dwells with you and will be in you" (vv. 16-17).

Jesus was saying, *When I go away, I will send Someone in my place, Someone just like Me who will walk alongside you just as I have done. And just as I have done, the Holy Spirit will assist, guide, and encourage you. What's more, He will not only walk beside you, He will live inside you.* As we progress through this study, we will

3

seek to deepen our relationship with this One who both walks beside and lives inside us.

This book is written as a sequel to my previous book, *Walking with the Apostles: Forty-five Days in the Book of Acts.* Like that book, this one was originally written as scripts for the Oral Learners Bible Institute (www.olbi.world). These scripts were designed to be read, recorded, and placed onto micro SD cards. These cards are then given to Majority World pastors and leaders to help prepare them for ministry. They insert the cards into their cell phones and listen to them. The title of the OLI course is "A Study of the Holy Spirit." Since these lessons were originally intended to train already serving pastors and church workers, they are designed to be very practical and formational.

How to Use This Book

You can read this book as one would any other nonfiction book, to gain more understanding on a given subject, in this case, the person and work of the Holy Spirit. However, I recommend that you read the book in a more profitable way, that is, as daily devotional. Or, as the subtitle of the book suggests, as a "thirty day journey of spiritual discovery." Your time spent in the book will thus become a month-long expedition whose purpose is not to merely to learn more about the Holy Spirit. Its purpose is to know Him better and to daily enter into His presence and experience His transforming power.

You will note that each lesson has two parts, *the reading,* which covers 3-4 pages, and *the application* at the end. The reading part will introduce you to some aspect of the Spirit's person and work as taught in Scripture. I recommend that you take your time and read deliberately and prayerfully.

The application part is found at the end of each day's reading under the heading "Walk with the Holy Spirit." You will note that this section has four parts: (1) a truth to embrace, (2) a commitment to make, (3) a prayer to pray, and (4) a verse to memorize. Take time to do each of these exercises. If you will, I promise you, your life will be transformed, as Paul promised, "And we, who with unveiled faces all reflect the Lord's glory, are being transformed into his likeness with ever-increasing glory, which comes from the Lord, who is the Spirit" (2 Cor. 3:18).

My hope is that once you complete this journey, at least four things will have happened in your life:

- You will better understand who the Holy Spirit is, including His essential nature and work.
- You will personally experience the Spirit's presence and power in your life.
- You will develop an intimate relationship with the Holy Spirit.
- You will be able to share the Spirit's blessings with others.

— Denzil R. Miller
Galatians 2:20

Introduction

Part 1

Who is the Holy Spirit?

Day 1

Introducing the Holy Spirit

In the New Testament Book of Acts is the story of a man named Simon. This man was a powerful sorcerer living in the city of Samaria. He would often astonish the people with his supernatural powers. Many followed him declaring, "This man is the Great Power of God!" Then one day Simon heard Philip the evangelist preaching about the kingdom of God and telling the people about Jesus. He believed Philip's message and began to follow him.

Soon after this, the apostles Peter and John came down from Jerusalem to Samaria. Simon watched them as they laid their hands on the new Samaritan Christians. To Simon's amazement, one by one the Holy Spirit came powerfully on each believer. Each one was dramatically filled with the Spirit—just as the 120 disciples had been on the Day of Pentecost.

Simon thought to himself, *In the past, I profited from peddling my cultic wares. If I had this power, I could use it to make even more money.* So, he made an offer to the apostles. "Sell me this power," he said, "so that, when I lay my hands on people, they too will receive the Holy Spirit."

When Peter heard this, he became angry. "May your money perish with you!" he said. "Do you really think you can buy and sell the power of the Holy Spirit?" Then, looking Simon straight in the eye, Peter ordered him, "Repent of your wickedness and ask God to forgive you." Simon was so shaken that he cried out in fear, "Peter, please pray for me that no awful thing will happen to me!"

Because Simon did not understand who the Holy Spirit is, and how He works, he made a grave mistake. Sadly, many today are making similar mistakes, and for similar reasons. This is but one reason we must learn what the Word of God teaches about the Holy Spirit.

In the coming days, we will be examining the person and work of the Holy Spirit. We will learn who He is, what He does, and how we should respond to Him. Our primary source of information about the Holy Spirit will be the Bible—the very book that He himself inspired. However, we will do more than study about Him; we will get to know Him. While it is important that we know about the Holy Spirit, it is equally important that we know Him personally and receive His power and direction in our lives.

Wrong Ideas about the Holy Spirit

Who then is the Holy Spirit? As with Simon the Sorcerer in our story, there is much misunderstanding on the subject. We will therefore begin our journey by clearing up a couple of false ideas about the Holy Spirit. One wrong idea is the vague notion that the Holy Spirit is some sort of ghost or disembodied spirit being. This idea could be reinforced by some older English translations of the Bible, such as the old King James Version, which refer to the Holy Spirit as the "Holy Ghost." While this was as a perfectly legitimate term when the KJV was published some 400 years ago, the word *ghost* has a different meaning to people today than it did back then.

Then it simply meant spirit. Today the word ghost speaks of the disembodied soul of a dead person who wanders among the living. This understanding of the Holy Spirit is far from what the Scriptures teach about the Holy Spirit.

Others think of the Holy Spirit as divine energy or impersonal spiritual force emanating from God. As such, the Spirit can be controlled and manipulated. We can thus use Him for our own purposes—much as a sorcerer or wizard would use his magical powers. This is apparently how Simon viewed the Holy Spirit. However, like the first idea, this idea about the Spirit of God is also false. Both ideas can lead to unhealthy, and even sinful, practices in the church.

How then does the Bible present the Holy Spirit?

The Holy Spirit is God

From Scripture we learn that the Holy Spirit is, in fact, God. Sometimes Bible scholars refer to Him as the "Third Person of the Godhead." This terminology can be a bit confusing. However, it need not be. When Bible scholars speak of the Godhead, they are talking about the very essence or nature of God. The Scriptures reveal God as a Trinity of being. In other words, He is "one God in three divine persons." He is God the Father, God the Son, and God the Holy Spirit. Paul spoke of the Trinity when he wrote, "May the grace of the Lord Jesus Christ, and the love of God, and the fellowship of the Holy Spirit be with you all" (2 Cor. 13:14). Jesus taught that we are to baptize new believers "in the name of the Father and of the Son and of the Holy Spirit" (Matthew 28:19). The point we are making here is that the Holy Spirit is in truth God.

As God, the Holy Spirit has all of the characteristics of God. For instance, He is eternal, all-powerful, all knowing, and everywhere present. He is holy, loving, faithful, and just. And, as God, He is sovereign. This means that He can never be controlled or manipulated. No person can ever command the Holy Spirit or use Him for their own purposes. As God, the Holy Spirit has supreme authority over all and the power and right to do as He pleases.

The Holy Spirit is a Person

Not only is the Holy Spirit God, He is a person. When we say that He is a person, we do not mean that He is a human being. We mean that, as a divine person, He thinks, feels, and wills.

He has a *mind*. Paul spoke of "the mind of the Spirit" who searches our hearts (Rom. 8:27). The Holy Spirit also has *feelings*. The Bible warns us against grieving the Holy Spirit: "And do not grieve the Holy Spirit of God, with whom you were sealed for the day of redemption." (Eph. 4:30). And the Spirit has a *will*. Paul told the Corinthian believers, "All these are empowered by one and the same Spirit, who apportions to each one individually as he wills" (1 Cor. 12:11, ESV).

It is therefore wrong to refer to the Holy Spirit as "it." We should always refer to the Holy Spirit as "He" or Him." And because He is a divine, loving person, we can live in intimate fellowship with Him. We will talk more about these things later. As we progress through this study, we will learn many wonderful truths about the Holy Spirit. For now, we should remember that He is God, and He wants to empower and help you.

Walking with the Holy Spirit

Now that you have concluded today's reading, take a few moments to complete the following exercise.

A Truth to Embrace: As the Third Person of the Godhead, the Holy Spirit is God. Because He is God, I must worship Him, and because He is a Person, I can know and love Him.

A Commitment to Make: I commit myself to understand the Holy Spirit and know Him better.

A Prayer to Pray: Dear Holy Spirit, as I begin this study about You, open my mind that I may know You and better understand Your ways.

A Verse to Memorize: "Therefore go and make disciples of all nations, baptizing them in the name of the Father and of the Son and of the Holy Spirit." (Matt. 28:19)

Day 1: Introducing the Holy Spirit

Day 2

Knowing the Holy Spirit

Have you ever met a person who, at first, you wondered if you would like them? However, as you came to know them better, you grew to love and highly respect them. That is how it should be with the Holy Spirit. The better we know Him, the more we come to love and honor Him.

Yesterday, we learned that the Holy Spirit is God. He is the "Third Person of the Trinity." We also learned that, because the Holy Spirit is a person, we can know Him and live in relationship with Him. The more we know about Him, the better we can know Him personally. One way the Bible reveals the Holy Spirit is through His names. Another way is through the symbols it uses to describe Him. Let's look at each of these ways.

Names of the Holy Spirit

The Scriptures ascribe to the Holy Spirit many names and titles. By reflecting on these names and titles, we can better understand His nature and work. Let's look at five of the important names given to the Spirit:

1. The Holy Spirit. First, the Bible calls Him the Holy Spirit. It uses this name 94 times, more than any other name. This name reminds us that God's Spirit is indeed holy. This means that He is utterly and totally untainted by sin and evil. He is the One who enables believers to live Christ-like, holy lives, fully dedicated to serving God.

2. The Spirit of God. Second, the Bible calls the Holy Spirit the Spirit of God. The Bible uses this name 25 times (for example, see Gen. 1:2: Rom. 8:14; Eph. 4:30). By calling the Holy Spirit the Spirit of God, the Bible is emphasizing His deity. He is, in fact, the Spirit who is God.

3. The Spirit of Christ. Third, the Bible sometimes refers to the Holy Spirit as the Spirit of Christ, or the Spirit of Jesus (see, Acts 16:7; Rom. 8:9; Phil. 1:19; 1 Pet. 1:11). This name reminds us of the Spirit's close relationship to Christ and His redemptive work. He is the One who anointed Jesus to fulfill His ministry. Moreover, He is the one who empowers believers to be Christ's witnesses "to the ends of the earth" (Acts 1:8).

4. The Spirit of Truth. Fourth, The Bible refers to the Holy Spirit as the Spirit of Truth. Speaking of the Holy Spirit, Jesus said, "When the Spirit of truth comes, he will guide you into all the truth" (John 16:13). As the Spirit of Truth, the Holy Spirit is the one who revealed Scripture to the prophets and apostles (2 Pet. 1:21). He will also guide us in understanding the truth found in Scripture.

5. The Helper. Fifth, Jesus called the Holy Spirit the Helper. He said, "I will ask the Father, and he will give you another Helper, to be with you forever" (John 14:16, ESV). The Holy Spirit is thus the One who "comes along side" believers to help, comfort, enable, and empower them to do God's will.

Symbols of the Holy Spirit

Just as the Scriptures use many names to describe the Holy Spirit, they also use many symbols to do the same. Let's look at six of those symbols:

1. A blowing wind. First, the Bible describes the Holy Spirit as a blowing wind (John 3:8; Acts 1:2). Jesus told Nicodemus, "The wind blows wherever it pleases... So it is with everyone born of the Spirit" (John 3:8). On the Day of Pentecost, the Spirit came as a sound from heaven "like the blowing of a violent wind" (Acts 2:3). Just as the wind is powerful and unable to be controlled, so is the almighty Spirit of God. He goes wherever He wants to execute and fulfill God's mission.

2. A blazing fire. Second, the Bible pictures the Holy Spirit as a blazing fire (Luke 3:16; Acts 1:3). John the Baptist introduced Jesus as the one who baptizes "with the Holy Spirit and with fire" (Luke 3:16). Then, on the Day of Pentecost, the Holy Spirit came as a "tongue of fire" and sat on the head of each of the 120 disciples (Acts 2:3). He is the One who will set our tongues aflame to proclaim the gospel to the ends of the earth.

3. A pouring rain. Third, the Bible depicts the Holy Spirit as a pouring rain (Joel 2:23-29). The prophet Joel said that God would one day pour out His Spirit on all flesh as "rains" and "abundant showers" (Joel 2:23). That outpouring began at Pentecost and will continue until Jesus comes again. On that Day of Pentecost, Peter announced, "This is what was spoken by the prophet Joel: 'In the last days, God says, I will pour out my Spirit on all people'" (Acts 2:16-17).

4. A flowing river. Fourth, the Bible pictures the Holy Spirit as a flowing river (John 7:37-39). Speaking of the Spirit, Jesus promised that the Spirit would one day flow through His followers as "rivers of living water" (v. 38, ESV). Believers are not to be mere containers of the Spirit. They are rather to be channels through which the Spirit flows giving life and blessing to others.

5. Anointing oil. Fifth, the Holy Spirit is compared with anointing oil (Acts 10:38; 1Jn. 2:20). In the Old Testament, prophets, priests, and kings were anointed with oil. This anointing indicated that the Spirit of the Lord had authorized and enabled them to fulfill their vocations. When Jesus began His ministry, He spoke of how the Spirit of the Lord was upon Him, anointing Him to accomplish His mission (Luke 4:18-19). John reminded his readers that they had "an anointing from the Holy One" (1 John 2:20). Today, when we are baptized in the Holy Spirit, He anoints and enables us to do God's work.

Finally, throughout Scripture the Holy Spirit is described as the *outstretched hand* (or finger) of God. Ezekiel described the Spirit's coming upon him as "the hand of the Lord" (Ezek. 37:1). In the New Testament, the powerful working of the Holy Spirit is sometimes described as the hand or finger of God. For instance, Jesus cast out demons "by the finger of God" (Luke 11:20; compare Matt. 12:28). And the "hand of the Lord" was with the Christians in Antioch empowering them to reach the lost (Acts 11:21). Today, the Spirit of the Lord still wants to stretch out His hand and work through His people, just as He did in the Book of Acts (Acts 4:30-31).

Walking with the Holy Spirit

Now that you have concluded today's reading, take a few moments to complete the following exercise.

A Truth to Embrace: I can know more about the nature and work of the Holy Spirit by prayerfully studying His names and symbols.

A Commitment to Make: I commit myself to better understand who the Holy Spirit is and how He works.

A Prayer to Pray: Dear Holy Spirit, fill me now, and help me to understand who You are and what You want to do in my life.

A Verse to Memorize: "And I will ask the Father, and he will give you another Helper, to be with you forever." (John 14:16, ESV)

Day 3

The Spirit of Missions

Someone has said that any organization rises or falls on the quality of its leadership. This truth applies to the church. Fortunately however, the church—that is, the true church—is not led by any man. The true church is led by Christ, through the Holy Spirit. Jesus founded the church. Then, when He went back to heaven, He sent the Holy Spirit to lead and guide it.

On Day 1, we learned that the Holy Spirit is God and that He is a Person. Then on Day 2, we examined some of the titles and symbols that the Scriptures use to represent Him. From these, we discovered, among other things, that the Spirit of God is holy, powerful, and sovereign—meaning that He has the right and the power to do whatever He pleases.

We further learned that, as the Spirit of Christ, the Holy Spirit has come to enable us to fulfill Christ's mission in the earth. Today, we will expand on this thought. We will talk about how the Holy Spirit is the "Spirit of Missions." As such, He fulfills three important missional roles: He is the Executive of the Godhead, the Director of the Harvest, and the Enabler of the Mission. Let's look more closely at each of these three roles.

Executive of the Godhead

First, the Holy Spirit is the Executive of the Godhead. When we say this, we do not mean that He is the boss of God. We rather mean that He is that member of the Trinity responsible to put God's plans into effect. He was sent by the Father and the Son to execute—or to carry out— God's mission in the earth.

Jesus once told His disciples, "I will ask the Father, and he will give you another Counselor [meaning the Holy Spirit] to be with you forever" (John 14:6). A few weeks later, when the Spirit was poured out on the Day of Pentecost, Peter stood up and explained to the crowd what had happened. He said that Jesus had been exalted to the right hand of God. There, He "received from the Father the promised Holy Spirit and has poured out what you now see and hear" (Acts 2:33). In other words, the Father and the Son have joined together to send the Spirit into the world to accomplish God's work.

Now, as Executive of the Godhead, the Holy Spirit is working in and through the church to carry out God's mission. He is moving in all the earth executing the will of the Father and the Son. Our job is to submit ourselves to the Spirit's leading, receive His power, and work with Him in fulfilling God's plan for the nations. Someone explained it this way: God the Father sent the Son; the Father and Son sent the Holy Spirit; and now, the Father, Son, and Holy Spirit send the church.

Director of the Harvest

Second, the Holy Spirit is the Director of the Harvest. Jesus once referred to himself as the "Lord of the Harvest." He instructed His disciples to "ask the Lord of the harvest...to send out workers into his harvest field" (Luke 10:2). Later, He told them that He was going to leave them and return to His Father. However, He would not leave them alone. He would send the Holy Spirit in His place to complete His work (John 14:16-18). Jesus began to fulfil this promise at Pentecost when He poured out His Spirit on His church. Now, the Holy Spirit has taken over Jesus' work and is now the "Director of the Harvest."

As Director of the Harvest, the Holy Spirit directs the work of missions. We see Him doing this throughout the Book of Acts. There, He calls people into the work. He then empowers them and directs them in the harvest field. Further, when they become discouraged or fearful, He comes to them and encourages them to carry on the work.

As the Spirit of Missions, the Holy Spirit will direct the harvest until the work is accomplished and Jesus comes again. That's why it is so important that every Christian be filled with, and remain full of, the Holy Spirit.

Enabler of the Mission Force

Finally, not only is the Holy Spirit the Executive of the Godhead and the Director of the Harvest, He is also the Enabler of the Missions Force. He is the one who empowers and equips the harvest workers to accomplish the task. Just before Jesus returned to heaven, He left His disciples with a final command and a final promise. His command was, "Do not leave Jerusalem, but wait for the gift my Father promised...for John baptized in water, but in a few days you will be baptized with the Holy Spirit" (Acts 1:4-5). His final promise was, "You will receive power when the Holy Spirit comes upon you, and you will be my witnesses in Jerusalem, and in all Judea and Samaria, and to the ends of the earth" (Acts 1:8).

Day 3: The Spirit of Missions

The disciples obeyed Jesus' command and received His promise. On the Day of Pentecost "they were all filled with the Holy Spirit and began to speak with other tongues as the Spirit enabled them" (Acts 2:4). As a result of this powerful spiritual experience known as the baptism in the Holy Spirit, they became effective witnesses of the gospel. The Book of Acts tells the exciting story of their Spirit-empowered ministries.

The Holy Spirit is indeed the Spirit of Missions. He will inspire, empower, guide, and sustain us in the mission. We will expand on these topics in upcoming days.

Walking with the Holy Spirit

Now that you have concluded today's reading, take a few moments to complete the following exercise.

A Truth to Embrace: I understand the Jesus gave the Holy Spirit to empower the church and to direct it to fulfill God's mission.

A Commitment to Make: I commit myself to do my part in fulfilling God's mission to redeem the nations.

A Prayer to Pray: God fill me now with Your missionary Spirit, and empower me to do Your will.

A Verse to Memorize: "The harvest is plentiful, but the workers are few. Ask the Lord of the harvest, therefore, to send out workers into his harvest field." (Luke 10:2)

Part 2

The Holy Spirit in the Old Testament

Day 4

The Creative Spirit

A Pentecostal pastor was once challenged by a non-Pentecostal colleague. "The problem with you Pentecostals," he said, "is that you don't believe that anything can happen until the Spirit moves!" "That's true," the Pentecostal pastor admitted. "In fact nothing in all history happened before the Spirit moved over the face of the waters, as is recorded in Genesis 1:2. Had the Spirit not moved, the world would not exist."

Yesterday, we learned that the Holy Spirit is the Spirit of Missions. One of His roles as the Spirit of Mission is that He serves as the Executive of the Godhead. By this, we mean that He is that member of the Trinity who is responsible to put God's plans into effect. Today, we will investigate two ways in the Old Testament that the Holy Spirit went about fulfilling the plan of God. We will discuss the Spirit's work in creating the universe. Then, we will discuss His work in creating and inspiring the Bible.

The Spirit Created the World

1. The Spirit who created. The first way that the Spirit went about fulfilling the plan of God was that He joined with the Father and the

Son in creating the universe. The first verse in the Bible says, "In the beginning God created the heavens and the earth" (Gen. 1:1). The next verse tells us how the Holy Spirit participated in this mighty work: "Now the earth was formless and empty, darkness was over the surface of the deep, and the Spirit of God was hovering over the waters." Centuries later, in the New Testament, John revealed that Jesus—whom he called "the Word"—also participated in creation (John 1:1-3). Thus, the Holy Spirit was there at the beginning working with the other members of the Trinity creating the heavens and the earth.

The Holy Spirit also participated in the creation of humankind. In Genesis 2 the Bible says that "the Lord God formed the man from the dust of the ground and breathed into his nostrils the breath of life, and the man became a living being" (v. 7). Job reveals that it was the life-giving Spirit of God who gave Adam life. He explains, "The Spirit of God has made me; the breath of the Almighty gives me life" (Job 33:4).

2. The Spirit who re-creates. Further, the same Holy Spirit who participated in the creation of the universe and the creation of humans, also participates in their *re-creation*. When Adam and Eve sinned, the loving fellowship they had with God was broken, and their natures were corrupted. They died spiritually. Since then, to be reunited with God, people need to be spiritually re-created.

On the night of His resurrection, Jesus appeared to His disciples in an upstairs room. He then "breathed on [or "into"] them and said, 'Receive the Holy Spirit'" (John 20:22). At that moment, they were recreated from the inside out. Jesus called this experience being "born again." He told Nicodemus "I tell you the truth, no one can see the kingdom of God unless he is born again.... Flesh gives birth to flesh, but the Spirit gives birth to spirit" (John 3:3-7).

The Holy Spirit regenerates us and gives us new life in Christ. Paul wrote, "Therefore, if anyone is in Christ, he is a new creation; the old has gone, the new has come!" (2 Cor. 5:17). To experience this new birth one must come to Christ, repent of his or her sins, and put their faith in Christ alone for salvation. Have you done that? If not, you can right now. Sincerely pray this prayer:

> "Jesus I come to You. I believe that You died on the cross for my sins, and that You rose again on the third day. I know that I am a sinner, and apart from faith in You, I am eternally lost. Please forgive me of my sins and become my Savior and Lord. I now forsake all my sins to follow You. Come into my heart and be Lord of my life. In Your name I pray. Amen."

The Spirit Created the Bible

The second way the Spirit worked in the Old Testament (and later in the New Testament) to fulfil God's mission was to inspire the Scriptures. He did this by moving on the prophets and the apostles, giving them the thoughts and words they wrote. Their Spirit-inspired words are found in our Bibles today.

1. The Holy Spirit inspired Scripture. Thus, the Holy Spirit is the true Author of the Bible. Peter explained it like this: "Above all, you must understand that no prophecy of Scripture came about by the prophet's own interpretation. For prophecy never had its origin in the will of man, but men spoke from God as they were carried along by the Holy Spirit" (2 Pet. 1:20-21). Note how "men spoke" as they were "carried along" by the Holy Spirit. Though the writers of Scripture often used their own words and terminology, they did so under the Spirit's inspiration and oversight. Therefore, Paul could write, "All Scripture is God-breathed [meaning Spirit-inspired] and is useful for teaching, rebuking, correcting and training in righteousness..."

(2 Tim. 3:16). Because the Bible is inspired by the Holy Spirit, it has power like no other book. It has power to open the heart, enlighten the mind, and convert the soul.

2. The Holy Spirit illuminates Scripture. While the Holy Spirit did indeed inspire the Word of God, He does even more. He comes to Christians and helps them to understand what is written. What a wonderful privilege. The very Author of the Bible will come to us and help us to understand the words He inspired. The Scriptures can only be fully understood with the help of the Holy Spirit. We will discuss this subject more on Day 23.

Walking with the Holy Spirit

Now that you have concluded today's reading, take a few moments to complete the following exercise.

A Truth to Embrace: Along with the Father and the Son, the Holy Spirit participated in the creation of the heavens and the earth. He also works in the lives of repentant sinners making them into new creations in Christ.

A Commitment to Make: I will yield myself to the Holy Spirit and allow Him to work in my life shaping me into the image of Christ.

A Prayer to Pray: Dear Holy Spirit, come inside me, and fill me now. Make me to be more like Jesus in all I say and do.

A Verse to Memorize: "Therefore, if anyone is in Christ, he is a new creation. The old has passed away; behold, the new has come." (2 Cor. 5:17)

Day 5

The Enabling Spirit

The Old Testament begins dramatically with the Spirit of God moving over the face of the deep. He is working with God the Father and God the Son creating the heavens and the earth (Gen. 1:1-2; John 1:3). This, however, is just the beginning of the Spirit's work in Scripture. Throughout the Old Testament, He worked on behalf of God's people. He enabled the leaders of His people to accomplish the work to which He had called them. Today, we will survey six of those ways.

Spirit-Produced Wonders

The first way the Spirit of the Lord worked on behalf of God's people in the Old Testament was through demonstrations of His mighty power. For instance, in Exodus, God's Spirit worked powerfully to deliver the children of Israel from Egyptian bondage. According to Jeremiah, the "Sovereign Lord" brought His people out of Egypt "with signs and wonders, by a mighty hand and an outstretched arm" (Jer. 32:21). You will remember from Day 2 that the outstretched arm of God is a symbol of the dynamic activity of the Holy Spirit. Isaiah adds that God brought His people through the sea by His Holy Spirit who was among them. The prophet wrote, "[By] his glorious arm of power.... [He] divided the waters before them" (Isa. 63:11-12). During that time, God also lead the Israelites "by a pillar of cloud by day and a pillar of fire by night" (Exo. 13:21-22). This fiery pillar is emblematic of the leadership and protection of the Holy Spirit over Israel.

Spirit-Enabled Leaders

The second way the Spirit worked on behalf of Israel was by enabling its leaders. Let's look at three examples:

1. The Spirit enabled Moses. God's Spirit worked in Moses, the great deliverer of the Israeli nation. God first appeared to him as "flames of fire from within a bush" (Exod. 3:2). From the bush, God told Moses that He had chosen him to deliver God's people from Egyptian bondage. As we learned on Day 2, this divine fire reminds us of the presence and power of the Holy Spirit. The Bible clearly states that the Spirit was on Moses (Num. 11:17).

2. The Spirit enabled the seventy elders. On one occasion, Moses was overwhelmed by the amount of work he had to do. God, however, provided him with an answer. He told Moses to gather seventy elders of Israel. Then, God "took some of the Spirit that was on [Moses] and put it on the seventy elders" (Num. 11:25). Immediately they began to prophesy. They were now ready to help Moses.

Joshua noticed that two men in the camp who had not gathered with the others also began to prophesy. He complained to Moses, saying, "My lord, stop them!" But, Moses replied, "I wish that all the Lord's people were prophets and that the Lord would put his Spirit on them!" (v. 29). This wish of Moses would one day be fulfilled on the

Day of Pentecost, when God began to pour out His Spirit on all flesh (Acts 2:17).

3. The Spirit enabled Joshua. Like Moses, Joshua was "a man in whom is the Spirit" (Num. 27:18). Because of this, Joshua was a great leader, and God did many mighty works through him enabling him to lead Israel to conquer the land of Canaan.

Spirit-Gifted Craftsmen

A third way the Spirit worked on behalf of God's people in the Old Testament was by giving craftsmen the skills they needed to do their work. In the wilderness God commissioned Moses to build the Tabernacle. It would serve as a place where His people could gather to worship Him. God told Moses to build the structure "exactly like the pattern I will show you" (Exod. 25:9). He then chose two men, Bezalel and Oholiab, to lead the project. God said to Moses, "I have filled [Bezalel] with the Spirit of God, with skill, ability and knowledge in all kinds of crafts" (Exod. 31:3). This story teaches us that the Spirit of God not only equips preachers and leaders to do their work, He also equips others, like craftsmen, to do to their work well.

Spirit-Endowed Judges

A fourth way the Spirit of the Lord helped the Israeli nation was to endow the Judges with military prowess. After Israel finally settled in the Promised Land, God raised up men and women known as "Judges." The Spirit anointed them to lead God's people in battles against their enemies. Let's look at four of those judges to see how the Holy Spirit worked through them.

1. Othniel was the first judge of Israel. The Bible says, "The Spirit of the Lord came upon him, so that he became Israel's judge and went to war" (Jdg. 3:10). Through the Spirit's power Othniel gained a great victory over Israel's enemies. After that, Israel enjoyed 40 years of peace.

2. Deborah was the only female judge. She was also a prophet (Jdg. 4:4). She prophesied that Israel would be victorious over their enemies. The Spirit then gave her a plan on how to defeat them. Following that plan, she urged Barak to lead an attack on the Canaanite forces of Sisera. Barak followed Deborah's instructions and gained the victory.

3. Gideon is perhaps Israel's most celebrated judge. His story is found in Judges 6-8. The Bible says that "the Spirit of the Lord clothed Gideon" empowering him to lead the armies of Israel to victory (6:34).

4. Samson is the most puzzling of the judges. At times, he did things contrary to God's will; nevertheless, the Spirit of God still used him. Once, when he was still a young man, "the Spirit of the Lord began to stir him" (13:35). Sometime later, Samson came upon a lion and "the Spirit of the Lord came upon him in power so that he tore the lion apart with his bare hands" (14:6). On another occasion, the Spirit came upon him again, and he struck down thirty of the enemies of Israel (14:19). On yet another occasion, the Spirit again came powerfully on him, and he slew a thousand Philistines with only the jawbone of a donkey (15:14-15).

The story of the Judges teaches us that God will empower His people by His Spirit to accomplish His work. We should always be open to the empowering work of the Spirit in our lives.

Spirit-Anointed Kings

The fifth way the Holy Spirit worked on behalf of God's people in the Old Testament was to anoint and enable Israel's kings to perform their duties. This is especially true for the nation's first two kings, Saul and David.

King Saul was the first king of Israel. When Samuel anointed him as king, God changed Saul's heart (1 Sam. 10:9). He then went to Gibeah where he met a group of prophets. As he drew near to them, "the Spirit of God came upon him in power, and he joined in their prophesying" (v. 10). This shows that Saul was truly anointed by the Holy Spirit. The Spirit of God then helped him win a great victory over the Ammonites (11:6-11). Sadly, however, Saul did not continue to follow God. Finally God withdrew His anointing from Saul and gave it to David (1 Sam. 16:13-14).

King David was a man who sought after God (1 Sam. 13:14), and God's Spirit dwelled in him. When Samuel anointed young David as king, the Bible says, "from that day on the Spirit of the Lord came upon David in power" (1 Sam. 16:13). Unlike others in the Old Testament, the Spirit remained upon David. He even became one of the writers of Scripture. Through the inspiration of the Holy Spirit, he wrote many of the Psalms in the Bible.

One time David committed a great sin. However, when the prophet challenged him, he quickly repented. David must have remembered how the Spirit had departed from Saul. So he prayed, "Create in me a pure heart, O God, and renew a steadfast spirit within me. Do not cast me from your presence or take your Holy Spirit from me" (Psa. 51:10).

We, like King David, should cherish the Spirit of God in our lives—and we should do nothing that will grieve the Holy Spirit and cause Him to depart from us.

Walking with the Holy Spirit

Now that you have concluded today's reading, take a few moments to complete the following exercise.

A Truth to Embrace: Just as He did with the Old Testament leaders and workers, the Spirit of God stands ready to anoint me and enable me to do the work God has assigned me to do.

A Commitment to Make: I commit myself seek God's Spirit for His guidance and enablement.

A Prayer to Pray: Holy Spirit come, fill me as You did Your servants in the Old Testament, and enable me to accomplish the work You have called me to do.

A Verse to Memorize: "So Samuel took the horn of oil and anointed him in the presence of his brothers, and from that day on the Spirit of the Lord came upon David in power." (1 Sam. 16:13)

Day 6

The Prophetic Spirit

Elijah and Elisha are good examples of how the Holy Spirit worked through the Old Testament prophets. By the Spirit's power, they declared the message of God and performed miracles. When Elijah's ministry was nearing its end, Elisha asked for a "double portion" of the Spirit that rested on his teacher. Then God took Elijah up to heaven in a whirlwind. As he went up, his mantle fell to the ground. This mantle symbolized the anointing of the Spirit that had been on the old prophet. Elisha picked up Elijah's mantle and walked to the bank of the Jordan River. With a loud voice, he cried out, "Where now is the Lord, the God of Elijah?" (2 Kings 2:14). He then struck the water with the mantle. At that, the river divided, and Elisha walked over to the other side. This showed that the Spirit of the Lord who had rested so powerfully on Elijah was now upon Elisha.

Today, we will look at how the Holy Spirit moved on and through the Old Testament prophets. One important way He used them was to reveal Scripture through them. The prophets further spoke of a day when God would pour out His Spirit on all people.

Let's look at three ways the Holy Spirit used the Old Testament prophets.

The Spirit Sent the Prophets

First, the Holy Spirit sent and empowered the prophets. Isaiah told how God had sent him. He testified, "The Sovereign Lord has sent me, endowed with his Spirit" (Isa. 48:16). The same thing could be said of all of the Hebrew prophets. They were all sent by the Holy Spirit, and they all ministered in the Spirit's power. Ezekiel testified, "[The Lord] said to me, 'Son of man, stand up on your feet and I will speak to you.' As he spoke, the Spirit came into me and raised me to my feet, and I heard him speaking to me. He said, 'Son of man, I am sending you to the Israelites...'" (Ezek. 2:1-3). Even the wicked King Nebuchadnezzar was able to see that the Spirit of God dwelt in the prophet Daniel (Dan. 4:8). All of the true Old Testament prophets were sent and empowered by Spirit of God.

The Spirit Spoke through the Prophets

Not only did the Holy Spirit send and empower the prophets, He spoke through them. King David—who was also a prophet—testified, "The Spirit of the Lord spoke through me; his word was on my tongue" (2 Sam. 23:1). Micah wrote, "But as for me, I am filled with power, with the Spirit of the Lord, and with justice and might, to declare to Jacob his transgression, to Israel his sin" (Micah 3:8). In other words, the prophets were filled with the Spirit to speak out against evil and to declare God's righteousness.

At times the Holy Spirit moved through the prophets inspiring them to write Scripture. Peter tells us how this came about. "Above all," he said, "you must understand that no prophecy of Scripture came about by the prophet's own interpretation. For prophecy never had its origin in the will of man, but men spoke from God as they were carried along by the Holy Spirit" (2 Pet. 1:20-21). In the New Testament, the Spirit spoke in the same way through the writings of the apostles. We therefore believe that "all Scripture is God-breathed" (2 Tim. 3:16), and that the entire Bible, both the Old and New Testaments, is the inspired Word of God and the revelation of God to man. Paul wrote the Christians in Thessalonica, saying, "We also thank God continually because, when you received the word of God, which you heard from us, you accepted it not as a human word, but as it actually is, the Word of God, which is indeed at work in you who believe" (1 Thess. 2:13).

The Prophets Told of the Spirit's Outpouring

The Old Testament prophets further spoke of a day when God would pour out His Spirit on all flesh. This universal outpouring would begin with the Spirit's coming upon the Messiah. Seven hundred years before the birth of Jesus the prophet Isaiah quotes the Messiah as saying, "The Spirit of the Sovereign Lord is on me, because the Lord has anointed me to preach good news to the poor. He has sent me to…proclaim the year of the Lord's favor" (Isa. 61:1-2). Jesus read from this very passage when He began His Messianic ministry (Luke 4:18-19). He then went out and fulfilled His ministry in the power of the Holy Spirit. We will talk more about this on Day 8.

Further, according to the prophets, the day was coming when the Lord would pour out the Spirit on all humanity. Under the Old Covenant, the Spirit was given only to certain prophets, priests, and leaders. And, He was given only at certain times to enable these leaders to perform certain tasks. However, the prophets told of a day when God would pour out His Spirit on all flesh. Speaking on God's behalf, Joel prophesied, "And afterward, I will pour out my Spirit on all people. Your sons and daughters will prophesy, your old men will dream dreams, your young men will see visions. Even on my servants, both men and women, I will pour out my Spirit in those days" (Joel 2:28-29).

That prophecy was first fulfilled on the Day of Pentecost when the ascended Lord poured out the Holy Spirit on the waiting believers. The Bibles says,

> "When the Day of Pentecost came, they were all together in one place. Suddenly a sound like the blowing of a violent wind came from heaven and filled the whole house where they were sitting. They saw what seemed to be tongues of fire that separated and came to rest on each of them. All of them were filled with the Holy Spirit and began to speak in other tongues as the Spirit enabled them." (Acts 2:1-4)

Peter then stood and explained what had happened. He said, "This is what was spoken by the prophet Joel: 'In the last days, God says, I will pour out my Spirit on all people.'" (Acts 2:16-17)

This ancient prophecy is still being fulfilled today. God is still pouring out His Spirit on anyone who will commit himself or herself to His mission and humbly seek His face. Jesus promised, "Your Father in heaven [will] give the Holy Spirit to those who ask him!" (Luke 11:13). Will you claim the promise today?

Walking with the Holy Spirit

Now that you have concluded today's reading, take a few moments to complete the following exercise.

A Truth to Embrace: I understand that the Old Testament prophets did not speak from their own minds but they spoke by the Spirit of God.

A Commitment to Make: I commit myself to yield my mind and thoughts to the Spirit and invite Him to speak to me.

A Prayer to Pray: Dear Holy Spirit, I open myself to You. Speak to me and work in me to accomplish Your will in my life.

A Verse to Memorize: "This is what was spoken by the prophet Joel: 'In the last days,' God says, 'I will pour out my Spirit on all people.'" (Acts 2:16-17)

Day 6: The Prophetic Spirit

Part 3

The Holy Spirit and Jesus

Day 7

The Spirit Prepared the Way

When we are expecting honored guests to come to our homes, we move into action. In preparation for their coming, we sweep the floors, make ready the guest room, and begin to plan and prepare the meals. We want to do everything we can to ensure that our guests have a pleasant stay.

The Holy Spirit did a similar thing in preparing the world for the coming of Jesus. He made everything ready so that the promised Messiah would be well received. Today, we will look at four ways the Holy Spirit prepared the world for the coming of Jesus. We will also look at how the Spirit works today, preparing people's hearts to receive Christ and be saved.

The Spirit Inspired the Prophets

The first way the Spirit prepared the world for Christ's coming was to send and inspire prophets to talk about Him. Centuries before He came, Spirit-inspired men revealed many details about Jesus' life and ministry. They did this to ensure that, when Messiah did come, He could be easily identified. For instance, Micah declared, "I am filled with power, with the Spirit of the Lord" (Mic. 3:8). He then predicted that the Messiah would be born in in the village of Bethlehem in the land Judea (5:2). Inspired by the Holy Spirit, Isaiah prophesied that the Christ would be born of a virgin (Isa. 7:14). Then as an adult, He would minister in the Spirit's power (61:1-2). The prophet further predicted that the Messiah would be rejected, beaten, crucified, and raised from the dead (53:3-10). These are but a few examples of the many details of Jesus' life that were foretold by the prophets. By comparing these Old Testament prophecies with the life of Christ as revealed in the New Testament, we know that Jesus is truly the Messiah, the Son of God and Savior of the world.

The Spirit Came Upon Mary

A second way the Spirit prepared the way for the coming Messiah was to come upon the virgin Mary and to cause her to miraculously conceive the Christ Child. The Bible says that before Mary and Joseph came together, "she was found to be with child through the Holy Spirit" (Matt. 1:18). An angel of the Lord explained to her, "The Holy Spirit will come upon you, and the power of the Most High will overshadow you. So the holy one to be born will be called the Son of God" (Luke 1:35). The same angel later encouraged Joseph, telling him, "Do not be afraid to take Mary home as your wife, because what is conceived in her is from the Holy Spirit. She will give birth to a son, and you are to give him the name Jesus, because he will save his people from their sins" (Matt. 1:20-21).

The Spirit Moved Upon Saints

A third way the Holy Spirit prepared the way for the arrival of the Messiah was to move on certain Judean saints and inspire them to rejoice at His coming. Soon after Mary conceived the Christ child, she went to visit her cousin, Elizabeth. Elizabeth was pregnant with John, the child who would grow to be John the Baptist. When

Elizabeth greeted Mary, the baby leaped in Elizabeth's womb and she was filled with the Holy Spirit. She then began to exclaim in a loud voice, "Blessed are you among women, and blessed is the child you will bear!" (Luke 1:41-42). At that, Mary was also filled with the Spirit and began to glorify the Lord (vv. 46-48).

Weeks later, when John was about to be born, the Holy Spirit came upon Zacharias, his father (v. 67). He announced that his child would be a prophet of the Most High God, and that he would prepare the way for the Lord (vv. 67-76).

During those same days, the Holy Spirit came to an old man named Simeon. The Spirit revealed to him that he would not die before he had seen the Lord's Christ. The day soon arrived when Joseph and Mary took the baby Jesus to the priests in the temple to be circumcised. The Spirit led Simeon into the temple courts. There, he took the baby Jesus in his arms and praised God, saying, "Lord, as you have promised, you may now dismiss your servant in peace. For my eyes have seen your salvation, which you have prepared in the sight of all people..." (Luke 2:30).

The Spirit Sent John the Baptist

The fourth way the Holy Spirit prepared the way for Jesus' coming was to send John the Baptist to announce His arrival. The Bible tells us that John was filled with the Spirit "even from birth" (Luke 1:15). Many years later, when John began His ministry, he came in the "Spirit and power of Elijah." The purpose of his coming was to "make ready a people prepared for the Lord" (v. 17). John identified Jesus in two ways: as "the Lamb of God who takes away the sin of the world," and as the One "who will baptize with the Holy Spirit" (John 1:29, 33). He told the people, "I baptize you with water. But one more powerful than I will come, the thongs of whose sandals

I am not worthy to untie. He will baptize you with the Holy Spirit and with fire" (Luke 3:16). Truly, the Holy Spirit was active preparing the world for the coming of the Messiah.

The Spirit Prepares Hearts

The Holy Spirit is still active in the world today preparing people for the coming of Christ. He works in their hearts getting them ready to receive Him as Savior. In the Book of Acts, when Paul and his missionary team arrived in the city of Philippi, they met a woman named Lydia. Paul shared the gospel with her. As he did, "the Lord opened her heart to respond to Paul's message" (Acts 16:14). Paul later wrote the Christians in Philippi, "For God is working in you, giving you the desire and the power to do what pleases him" (Phil. 2:13, NLT).

Nothing pleases God more that people opening the hearts to Christ and following Him as Lord and Savior. The Spirit prepares people's hearts by revealing Christ to them, convicting them of their sin, and imparting the faith they need to believe on Christ and be saved. We will discuss this work of the Spirit in more detail on Day 15.

Walking with the Holy Spirit

Now that you have concluded today's reading, take a few moments to complete the following exercise.

A Truth to Embrace: I understand that the Spirit worked preparing the world for the coming of Jesus the Messiah, and He still works in people's hearts preparing them to receive Christ as Savior.

A Commitment to Make: I commit myself to pray for lost people, asking the Holy Spirit to open their hearts to the message of Christ.

A Prayer to Pray: Dear Holy Spirit, I pray that You will move on the hearts of my unsaved loved ones calling them to salvation.

A Verse to Memorize: "For God is working in you, giving you the desire and the power to do what pleases him." (Phil. 2:13, NLT)

Day 8

The Spirit Empowered Jesus

In previous lessons, we have learned how the Holy Spirit anointed and enabled the Old Testament prophets, kings, and craftsmen to accomplish the work God gave them. Today, we will learn how the Spirit anointed and empowered Jesus, the Messiah, to fulfill His ministry.

Someone may ask, "Why would Jesus need the power of the Holy Spirit? Wasn't He the eternal Son of God manifested in the flesh?" The answer is that, indeed, Jesus was—and is—the eternal Son of God. Had He chosen, He could have done all of His mighty works in His own divine power. Jesus, however, chose not to minister in this way. He rather chose to minister as a man empowered by the Holy Spirit. To fully understand this truth, one must understand four other biblical truths.

Jesus Humbled Himself

First, we must understand how *Jesus humbled himself.* The Bible teaches that when Jesus came to earth, He chose to "empty" Himself of His divine power and rights so that He might truly live, minister, and die on the cross as a man. In his letter to the Philippians, Paul explained how Christ possessed the "very nature of God." However, He "did not consider equality with God something to be used to his own advantage; rather, he made himself nothing by taking the very nature of a servant." In other words, the Son of God became a common man. Paul continues, "And being found in appearance as a man, he humbled himself [or "emptied Himself," NASB] by becoming obedient to death—even death on a cross!" (Phil. 2:5-8). In other words, Jesus humbled himself by denying himself of His privileges and powers as the Son of God. He willingly chose to live and minister as a man. He did this so that He could be our example of how we too could live and minister in the Spirit's power.

Jesus Was Empowered by the Spirit

The second truth we must understand is that *Jesus Christ, the Messiah, was anointed and empowered by the Holy Spirit.* In fact, the Hebrew word translated *Messiah*, and the Greek word translated *Christ*, have the same meaning. They both mean the "Anointed One."

Jesus was anointed by the Holy Spirit at His baptism in the Jordan River. There, He actually received two baptisms. He was first baptized in water. Then, He was baptized in the Holy Spirit. The Bibles says, "Jesus was baptized" in water. Then, "as he was praying, heaven was opened and the Holy Spirit descended on him in bodily form like a dove" (Luke 3:21-22). As a result, Jesus was empowered by the Holy Spirit to fulfill His ministry.

Jesus Ministered by the Spirit

Third, we must understand how *Jesus fulfilled His ministry in the Spirit's power.* Soon after He was baptized, Jesus went to a synagogue in Galilee. There, He described what happened to Him when the Spirit came upon Him. "The Spirit of the Lord is on me," He said, "because he has anointed me to preach good news to the poor. He has sent me to proclaim freedom for the prisoners and recovery of sight for the blind, to release the oppressed, to proclaim the year of the Lord's favor" (Luke 4:18-19).

Luke tells us that, as soon as Jesus was anointed by the Spirit, "he began his ministry" (3:23). He then "returned to Galilee in the power of the Spirit" (4:14). Being full of the Spirit, He proclaimed the good news, healed the sick, and cast out demons. Everyone was "amazed at the gracious words that came from his lips" (4:22). As Jesus taught, "the power of the Lord was present for him to heal the sick" (5:17). Peter summed up Jesus' ministry like this: "God anointed Jesus of Nazareth with the Holy Spirit and power, and…he went around doing good and healing all who were under the power of the devil, because God was with him" (Acts 10:38).

The Bible tells us that Jesus even died on the cross and rose again through the power of the Holy Spirit. It says that Jesus "through the eternal Spirit offered himself unblemished to God" (Heb. 9:14). Then, the same Holy Spirit who sustained Jesus on the cross raised Him from the dead (Rom. 8:11). Jesus thus performed His entire ministry in the power of the Spirit.

Jesus is Our Model for Ministry

Finally, we must understand that *God expects us to carry out our ministries in the same way Jesus carried out His ministry—in the power of the Holy Spirit.* Jesus chose to minister as a man full of the Holy Spirit so He could be our model. The night before His crucifixion, Jesus promised His disciples, "Anyone who has faith in me will do what I have been doing. He will do even greater things than these, because I am going to the Father" (John 14:12). He then told them what He would do when He arrived at His Father's side.

"I will ask the Father," He said, "and he will give you another Counselor to be with you forever—the Spirit of truth" (vv.16-17).

Jesus first fulfilled this promise on the Day of Pentecost. Since that time, we, like Jesus, can be empowered by the Spirit. We can preach and teach with power, and we can be used by God to heal the sick and challenge and defeat demonic spirits. And like Jesus, we can endure hardship and persecution and finish the work the Lord has given us to do.

Walking with the Holy Spirit

Now that you have concluded today's reading, take a few moments to complete the following exercise.

A Truth to Embrace: Like Jesus, I too can be anointed by the Holy Spirit and empowered to fulfill my God-given ministry.

A Commitment to Make: I commit myself to living my life and fulfilling my ministry in the Spirit's power.

A Prayer to Pray: Lord Jesus, fill me with the Holy Spirit and empower me to do the work You have given me.

A Verse to Memorize: "How God anointed Jesus of Nazareth with the Holy Spirit and with power. He went about doing good and healing all who were oppressed by the devil, for God was with him." (Acts 10:38)

Day 9

Jesus Promised the Spirit

To build an effective organization leaders must not only themselves be competent, they must instill that same competency into the lives of their team. This is what Jesus did. He promised to give them the same Holy Spirit who empowered and enabled Him in ministry.

Yesterday, we discussed how Jesus ministered in the Spirit's power. He preached and taught by the Spirit's inspiration, and He did His mighty works—such as healing the sick and casting out demons—in the Spirit's power. Peter put it this way: "God anointed Jesus of Nazareth with the Holy Spirit and power, and...he went around doing good and healing all who were under the power of the devil, because God was with him" (Acts 10:38).

Today, we will look at how Jesus promised that same power to His followers. He did this on at least four occasions. Let's look at each of these four great promises of the Spirit. In doing this, we will examine what Jesus said and what those sayings mean to us today.

Jesus Promised "Streams of Living Water"

First, Jesus promised His followers "streams of living water." He was in Jerusalem during the celebration of the Feast of Tabernacles. On the final day of the feast, Jesus stood in the temple court and cried out, "If anyone is thirsty, let him come to me and drink. Whoever believes in me, as the Scripture has said, streams of living water will flow from within him" (John 7:37-38). John explained that Jesus was talking about the Holy, whom those who believed in Him would receive. The Spirit's power would flow through them touching the lives of others. This promise was fulfilled on the Day of Pentecost and on many other occasions in the Book of Acts.

Today, the Spirit will do the same in us. He will freely flow in and through anyone who will sincerely seek the Lord. Jesus promised, "Your Father in heaven [will] give the Holy Spirit to those who ask him!" (Luke 11:13).

Jesus Promised "Another Helper"

Jesus gave a second promise concerning the Holy Spirit. This happened in an upper room in Jerusalem on the evening before His death. He told His disciples that He would soon leave them. However, He would not leave them alone. He would send the Holy Spirit to take His place as their Helper and Guide.

"I will pray the Father," Jesus said, "and He will give you another Helper, that He may abide with you forever, even the Spirit of truth…" (John 14:16-17, ESV).

Jesus then explained what this would mean to them. "I tell you the truth," He said, "anyone who has faith in me will do what I have been doing. He will do even greater things than these, because I am going to the Father" (v.12).

Jesus thus promised that, when the Helper came, He would do two things. He would live inside them, and He would empower them to do the kind of things Jesus himself did while He was here on earth. The Helper is the Holy Spirit, and He will do the same for us today. He will come to us and assist us in our walk with Christ and in our ministries for Him.

Jesus Promised to Be with Us

Several days later, Jesus gave a third promise concerning the Holy Spirit. On the night of His resurrection, He appeared to His disciples. After greeting them, He charged them, saying, "As the Father has sent me, I am sending you." Then, He did a remarkable thing. "He breathed on (or into) them and said, 'Receive the Holy Spirit'" (John 20:21-22). For the disciples, this experience represented both a present reality and a future promise. At that moment they received the Spirit—they were born of the Spirit. However, Jesus was also speaking of the future. He was promising to empower them with the Spirit on the coming Day of Pentecost.

Jesus issued His "Great Commission" at least three more times during the next forty days. Each time He gave the Commission, He promised the Spirit's presence or power. For example, in the gospel of Matthew Jesus commissioned His disciples to "go and make disciples of all nations." Jesus then ended His Commission with a wonderful promise. He said, "And surely I am with you always, to the very end of the age" (Matt. 28:18-20). This was a promise of the Holy Spirit. Jesus was saying that He would be with them in presence of the Holy Spirit as He had earlier promised in the upper room. Even today, Jesus is with every born-again Christian through His indwelling Spirit.

Jesus Promised Power to Witness

In Acts 1:8 Jesus promised the Spirit a fourth time. This is Jesus' final promise to His church, which He gave just before He ascended into heaven. In this promise, Jesus said to His disciples, "You will receive power when the Holy Spirit comes on you; and you will be my witnesses in Jerusalem, and in all Judea and Samaria, and to the ends of the earth." Jesus had given them a job to do—the evangelization of the nations. It was a job beyond their human abilities and could only be accomplished in the Spirit's power. Jesus therefore commanded them to "stay in the city until you have been clothed with power from on high" (Luke 24:19).

Jesus' final promise and command still apply to us today. We have inherited the first disciples' job of taking the gospel to the ends of the earth. It is therefore essential that we, like they, be empowered as Christ's witnesses. We too must obey Christ's command to receive the promise of the Holy Spirit.

Walking with the Holy Spirit

Now that you have concluded today's reading, take a few moments to complete the following exercise.

A Truth to Embrace: Jesus has promised to give His Spirit to me to empower me to serve Him more perfectly.

A Commitment to Make: I commit myself to daily seek the Spirit's power and presence in my life.

A Prayer to Pray: Jesus, I claim Your promise of the Spirit's power and presence in my life. Come Holy Spirit; fill me now.

A Verse to Memorize: "But you will receive power when the Holy Spirit has come upon you, and you will be my witnesses in Jerusalem and in all Judea and Samaria, and to the end of the earth." (Acts 1:8)

Day 10

Jesus Poured Out the Spirit

I n this world, we are accustomed to people not keeping their promises. Because of this, we are sometimes tempted to doubt God's promises. However, we can be confident that God will always keep His promises.

That's what happened on the Day of Pentecost; Jesus kept one of His most important promises. As we discovered yesterday, on four separate occasions, Jesus promised His disciples that He would send the Holy Spirit upon them. It was at Pentecost that He first fulfilled those promises.

The Promise is Fulfilled

The story of the outpouring of the Holy Spirit at Pentecost is found in the Bible in Acts 2. Luke describes the scene like this: After Jesus returned to heaven, the apostles went back to Jerusalem and told the others about Jesus' promise. They then set themselves to prayer. About a week later, on the Day of Pentecost, 120 of Jesus' most committed followers gathered in the temple court to wait on the Lord. That's when things began to happen.

Suddenly, there came from heaven a sound like the roaring of a mighty windstorm. The deafening noise filled the entire temple complex where thousands had gathered to celebrate the Feast of Harvest. Suddenly, what looked like a great mass of fire appeared over the heads of the 120 disciples. The flaming mass then divided itself into 120 "tongues of fire" and one settled above the head of each disciple. Then, the Holy Spirit, who was upon them, rushed inside them, and "all of them were filled with the Holy Spirit and began to speak in other tongues as the Spirit enabled them" (Acts 2:4). When the multitudes saw what was happening, they rushed to where the 120 had gathered. In wonder, they cried out, "What does this mean?"

Peter stood and explained to the crowd that they were witnessing a fulfilment of Joel's ancient prophecy: "In the last days, God says, I will pour out my Spirit on all people" (Acts 2:17). This outpouring of the Spirit was further a fulfillment of Jesus promise to His disciples: "In a few days you will be baptized with the Holy Spirit" (v. 5). Peter continued his message: "God has raised this Jesus to life, and we are all witnesses of the fact. Exalted to the right hand of God, he has received from the Father the promised Holy Spirit and has poured out what you now see and hear" (vv. 32-33).

The Church is Empowered

As you will remember, in yesterday's lesson we learned how Jesus left His followers an amazing promise. Just before He ascended into heaven, He told them, "But you will receive power when the Holy Spirit comes on you; and you will be my witnesses in Jerusalem, and in all Judea and Samaria, and to the ends of the earth" (Acts 1:8).

Now, on the Day of Pentecost, immediately upon receiving the Spirit, the disciples began to witness with power, just as Jesus had promised. Peter stood and preached. His Spirit-anointed words so pierced the hearts of all who heard him that they cried out, "What must we do?" Peter told them to repent and be baptized in Jesus' name, and they too could receive the gift of the Holy Spirit. Amazingly, 3,000 obeyed Peter's instructions and committed themselves to the Lord Jesus.

Not only did Peter witness with power, so did the others who received the Spirit on the Day of Pentecost. Because of their witness, "the Lord added to their number daily those who were being saved" (v.47). This same *empowering-results-in-witness* pattern is repeated throughout the Book of Acts. On numerous occasions the Holy Spirit comes upon and fills disciples. Each time, they are enabled to witness with great power and effectiveness.

The Gift is for All

We must not think, however, that this divine empowering was just for those early disciples. It is for every follower of Jesus until He returns from heaven. We all need the Spirit's power because we have all been called to be Christ's witnesses. On the Day of Pentecost, Peter told the crowd, "The promise [of the Holy Spirit] is for you and your children and for all who are far off—for all whom the Lord our God will call" (v. 39).

Like those first disciples, we must each personally experience that divine empowering. The Bible teaches that we receive the Holy Spirit by asking in faith. Jesus taught that our "Father in heaven [will] give the Holy Spirit to those who ask him!" (Acts 11:13). Paul added that we receive the promise of the Spirit by faith (Gal. 3:14).

Walking with the Holy Spirit

Now that you have concluded today's reading, take a few moments to complete the following exercise.

A Truth to Embrace: Jesus first poured out the Spirit on the Day of Pentecost, and He continues to pour out His Spirit on receptive hearts today.

A Commitment to Make: I commit to live in such a way that the Spirit's presence may rest on me.

A Prayer to Pray: Lord Jesus, create in me a heart that hungers for You and Your Spirit.

A Verse to Memorize: "Create in me a pure heart, O God, and renew a steadfast spirit within me. Do not cast me from your presence or take your Holy Spirit from me." (Psa. 51:10-11, a prayer of King David).

Part 4

The Holy Spirit and the
Mission of God

Day 11

The Holy Spirit Gives Life
to the Church

A fine car is a wonderful thing. However, without fuel the car is useless. It cannot perform the function for which it was created. It is the same with a church. A large gathering of people on Sunday morning may be very impressive. However, without the presence and power of the Holy Spirit that church has no life. It cannot perform the function for which it was created—no matter how wonderful it may appear from the outside. The Spirit alone gives life to any church. Today, we will look at five ways the Holy Spirit works in the church to give to it the vigor it needs to fulfill its God-ordained work in the world.

The Spirit Indwells the Church

The first way the Holy Spirit gives life to the church is by indwelling it. Wherever the Spirit of the Lord is, there is life. And where He is not, there is no life. He is, indeed, the Spirit of Life. Jesus put it this way, "The Spirit gives life; the flesh counts for nothing" (John 6:63). Paul wrote the church in Corinth and reminded them,

"Don't you know that you yourselves are God's temple and that God's Spirit dwells in your midst?" (1 Cor. 3:16). As the Spirit of the Lord fills the church, He gives to it divine life and purpose.

How then does the Spirit indwell the church? He indwells the church by indwelling its true members, those who have been born of the Spirit, those who have totally committed themselves to Jesus Christ and His mission.

The Spirit Baptizes Believers into the Church

A second way the Holy Spirit gives life to the church is by adding newly regenerated believers to the church. When someone repents of their sins and receives Christ as Savior, the Holy Spirit comes inside them. He then places them into the body of Christ. They become "living stones" in God's spiritual building (1 Pet. 2:5). Paul wrote, "For by one Spirit we were all baptized into one body, whether Jews or Greeks, whether slaves or free, and we were all made to drink of one Spirit" (1 Cor. 12:13). This is what happened in the Book of Acts. As people heard the good news and believed, "the Lord added to their number daily those who were being saved" (Acts 2:47). Everyone who has been truly born again is part of the body of Christ, the church.

The Spirit Empowers the Church for Witness

A third way the Spirit gives life to the church is by empowering its members as Christ's witnesses. Jesus promised His disciples, "You will receive power when the Holy Spirit comes on you; and you will be my witnesses..." (Acts 1:8). The church exists to bear witness to Christ and His saving work and to "make disciples of all nations" (Matt. 28:19). It can only do this work in the Spirit's power. This is why it is essential that every follower of Christ be empowered by the

Holy Spirit. We will discuss this essential work of the Holy Spirit more in tomorrow's lesson.

The Spirit Inspires True Worship

A fourth way the Holy Spirit gives life to the church is by inspiring God's people to worship Him. When followers of Jesus respond to the Spirit, He lifts their hearts in true spiritual worship. Jesus said, "God is spirit, and those who worship Him must worship in spirit and truth" (John 4:24). Paul described the church as those "who worship by the Spirit of God, who glory in Christ Jesus, and who put no confidence in the flesh" (Phil. 3:3).

In another place, the apostle explained how we are to worship by the Spirit. He said, "When you come together, everyone has a hymn, or a word of instruction, a revelation, a tongue or an interpretation" (1Cor.14:26). All of these activities are to be carried out as the Spirit fills and prompts believers gathered in worship. A worship service is only truly "lively" when the Spirit fills and inspires God's people to worship Him in Spirit and truth.

The Spirit Gives Gifts to the Church

A final way the Holy Spirit enlivens the church is by giving spiritual gifts to God's people. Paul said that God gives these gifts "to each one…for the common good" (1 Cor. 12:7). These gifts include revelation gifts, given "that we might "know the mind of God"; prophetic gifts, given "that we might speak the words of God"; and power gifts given "that we might do the works of God."

These spiritual gifts have two purposes. First, they are given to build up and strengthen the church. Paul talks about this in his first letter to the Corinthians. Secondly, they are given to enable the church to fulfill its evangelistic mission. We see this happening throughout the Book of Acts. We will discuss spiritual gifts more on Day 29. For now, it is important to understand that these gifts are one way the Spirit gives life and strength to the church.

Walking with the Holy Spirit

Now that you have concluded today's reading, take a few moments to complete the following exercise.

A Truth to Embrace: Without the power and presence of the Holy Spirit a church is destined to be weak and ineffectual.

A Commitment to Make: I commit myself to pray that God will pour out His Spirit on my church.

A Prayer to Pray: Holy Spirit, come and fill me and make me a channel through which You can flow to bless and enliven my church.

A Verse to Memorize: "God is spirit, and those who worship Him must worship in spirit and truth." (John 4:24)

Day 12

The Holy Spirit Empowers Us for Mission

I t is one thing to want to do something good; it is quite another thing to have the power do it. Yesterday, we discussed how Jesus promised His disciples the power they needed to accomplish the work He had given them. He said, "You will receive power when the Holy Spirit comes on you; and you will be my witnesses in Jerusalem, and in all Judea and Samaria, and to the ends of the earth" (Acts 1:8). Today, we will expand on this topic. We will look at five ways the Spirit empowers us to fulfill God's mission.

The Spirit Compels Us to Witness

The first way the Spirit empowers us to fulfill God's mission is that *He compels us to witness* to the lost about Christ. With the baptism in the Holy Spirit comes an inner compulsion to tell others about Jesus and His salvation. When Peter and John were ordered to stop preaching and teaching in Jesus' name, they replied, "We cannot help speaking about what we have seen and heard" (Acts 4:20). The Holy Spirit was in them compelling them to talk about their Lord.

Thousands today could share similar testimonies. When they were filled with the Spirit, they began to see people in a new way. They suddenly wanted them to know Christ as they knew Him. In the same way, the Spirit compels us to tell others about Jesus.

The Spirit Enables Us to Speak

The second way the Spirit empowers us for mission is that *He enables us to preach and teach* with greater power and effectiveness. In the Book of Acts, once the disciples were filled with the Spirit, they spoke with unexpected ability. The people were astonished that these ordinary men spoke with such authority. For example, Peter was an uneducated fisherman. Yet, after he received the Spirit on the Day of Pentecost, he stood and preached with power. The people were "cut to the heart" as they listened to his words (Acts 2:37). As a result, 3,000 people repented and committed their lives to Christ.

Concerning the apostles preaching, the Bible says, "With great power the apostles continued to testify to the resurrection of the Lord Jesus, and much grace was upon them all" (4:33). We can have that same "great grace" upon our lives if we will be empowered by the Holy Spirit as they were.

The Spirit Equips Us to Defeat Demons

A third way the Spirit enables us in mission is that *He equips us to challenge and defeat demonic powers.* Satan and his demons strongly oppose the proclamation of the gospel. Paul wrote, "The god of this age [Satan] has blinded the minds of unbelievers, so that they cannot see the light of the gospel of the glory of Christ" (2 Cor. 4:4).

Jesus overcame demons in the Spirit's power, and so must we. He testified, "I drive out demons by the Spirit of God" (Matt. 12:28). Then, when He issued His Great Commission, He declared, "These signs will accompany those who believe: In my name they will drive out demons…" (Mark 16:17). This is yet another reason we must be filled with—and remain full of—the Holy Spirit.

The Spirit Empowers Us to Work Miracles

A fourth way the Spirit equips us for mission is that *He empowers us to work miracles* in Jesus' name. In Acts, signs and wonders were a key element in advancing the gospel. Following the Spirit's outpouring at Pentecost, "awe came upon every soul, and many wonders and signs were being done through the apostles" (2:43). Paul testified that he won the Gentiles to Christ "by the power of signs and miracles, through the power of the Spirit" and by "fully proclaim[ing] the gospel of Christ" (Rom. 15:18-19).

Not only did the Spirit work through the apostles, He also worked through Spirit-filled laymen such as Stephen and Philip. The Bible says that Stephen was "full of grace and power [and] was doing great wonders and signs among the people" (Acts 6:8). It says about Philip, "The crowds with one accord paid attention to what was being said by Philip when they heard him and saw the signs that he did" (8:6).

The same can be true today. If we will be filled with the Spirit and remain committed to God's mission, the Spirit will work through to us to perform miracles to the glory of God.

The Spirit Gives Us Courage

The fifth way the Spirit empowers us for mission is that *He gives us courage* to witness for Christ in the face of danger and threats. Proclaiming Christ can be a dangerous business. Stephen was stoned for his witness, James was beheaded, and Peter was imprisoned for proclaiming Christ. And Paul was once stoned and left for dead.

Nevertheless, because these men were full of the Holy Spirit, they continued to proclaim Christ in the face of persecution.

When we face hostility and threat today, we must be like those first Christians. We must be filled with the Spirit and continue to boldly proclaim the message of salvation.

Walking with the Holy Spirit

Now that you have concluded today's reading, take a few moments to complete the following exercise.

A Truth to Embrace: If I will commit myself to God's mission, and be filled with the Holy Spirit, He will inspire and embolden me to witness for Christ.

A Commitment to Make: I commit to living a Spirit-empowered life focused on doing my part to tell others about Christ and His salvation.

A Prayer to Pray: Dear Holy Spirit, fill me now; compel, empower, and embolden me to witness for Christ.

A Verse to Memorize: "After they prayed, the place where they were meeting was shaken. And they were all filled with the Holy Spirit and spoke the word of God boldly." (Acts 4:31)

Day 13

The Spirit Directs Us
in the Mission

Today we have detailed maps, and even GPS devices, to help direct us to where we want to go. However, no map or device can tell us where God wants us to go. Only the Spirit of God can do that. In Scripture, we read of the Spirit of God choosing and sending people into the harvest. He then directs them to where He wants them to go and shows them what He wants them to do.

You will remember that on Day 3 we learned that Jesus is the "Lord of the Harvest" (Matt. 9:8). While here on earth, He directed the work of missions. He once told His disciples, "Do you not say, 'Four months and then the harvest'? I tell you, open your eyes and look at the fields! They are ripe for harvest" (John 4:35). However, just before He returned to heaven, Jesus promised to send the Holy Spirit to take His place. Now, since the Day of Pentecost, the Holy Spirit has served as Director of the Harvest.

As the Director of the Harvest, the Holy Spirit performs at least three essential missionary tasks: He *calls* people to the work, He *sends* them into the fields, and He *guides* them in the work of harvesting. Let's look more closely at these three ways the Holy Spirit actively directs the harvest.

The Spirit Calls

The first way the Spirit directs the harvest is by calling people to labor in the fields. In Old Testament times, the Spirit called and empowered the prophets to fulfill their vocations. Micah could have been speaking for any of the prophets when he wrote, "But as for me, I am filled with power, with the Spirit of the Lord" (Mic. 3:8).

In the New Testament, Jesus began His ministry by choosing and calling His apostles. These twelve divinely selected men were to follow Him, learn from Him, and eventually take on the ministry He began (Luke 9:1). He told them, "You did not choose me, but I chose you and appointed you to go and bear fruit—fruit that will last" (John 15:16).

Since Pentecost, the Holy Spirit has assumed Jesus' role as Director of the Harvest. He is now the one who calls men and women into the Lord's service. He calls *some* to special tasks. However, He calls *all* to participate in God's mission of redeeming lost humanity. Our responsibility is to be filled with the Spirit, open to His voice, and ready to say "Yes!" when the Spirit speaks.

The Spirit Sends

Second, the Spirit sends laborers into the harvest fields. Isaiah the prophet testified, "The Lord God, and his Spirit, have sent me (Isa. 48:16, KJV). In the New Testament, when it was time for Paul to begin his missionary ministry, the Holy Spirit moved in the church at Antioch where he and Barnabas were teaching. Speaking through a prophet, the Spirit said, "Set apart for me Barnabas and Saul for the

work to which I have called them" (Acts 13:2). The elders of the
church then laid hands on them and sent them off. Luke then notes
that they were "sent off by the Holy Spirit" (v. 4).

It is the same today. The Spirit still sends committed men and
women into the fields to labor in God's end-time harvest.

The Spirit Guides

Not only does the Holy Spirit call people into God's harvest; and
not only does He send them on their way, He further guides them in
the work. He tells them were to go and what do to once they arrive at
their place of ministry.

Jesus is our example in ministry. He himself was guided by the
Holy Spirit. When He was baptized in the Jordan River, the Spirit of
God came upon Him. Then, He was "led by the Spirit into the desert"
(Luke 4:1). The Spirit continued to guide Jesus throughout His
ministry.

The Holy Spirit also guided Jesus' followers in the Book of Acts.
For example, the Spirit of God guided Philip to the Gaza Road to
share Christ with an Ethiopian nobleman (Acts 8:29). He further
guided Paul and his missionary team into Macedonia. First, the Holy
Spirit stopped them from going westward into the province of Asia.
Then, He would not allow them to go northward to Bithynia. Finally,
the Holy Spirit gave Paul a vision in the night. In this vision, Paul saw
a man from Macedonia standing and begging him, "Come over to
Macedonia and help us!" Paul and his team then knew that God
wanted them to go to Europe to preach the good news there (16:6-10).
Paul would later write, "Those who are led by the Spirit of God are
the children of God" (Rom. 8:14).

The Spirit still wants to direct us in our ministries today.
Sometimes He will give us dreams and visions as He did Peter and

Paul. However, He most often directs us through deep inner promptings. He says to us, "This is the way; walk in it" (Isa. 30:21).

Walking with the Holy Spirit

Now that you have concluded today's reading, take a few moments to complete the following exercise.

A Truth to Embrace: I can trust the Holy Spirit to direct and guide me in the ministry Christ has given me.

A Commitment to Make: I will remain committed to God's will for my life, and I will listen for the Spirit's voice to direct me.

A Prayer to Pray: Dear Holy Spirit, I submit myself to You and to God's will. Now direct me to what You want me to do.

A Verse to Memorize: "Those who are led by the Spirit of God are the children of God." (Rom. 8:14)

Day 14

The Spirit Enables Us
to Represent Christ

Someone has rightly pointed out that in Acts 1:8 Jesus did not say "You will receive power…and you will witness *for* me." He rather said, "You will receive power… and you will *be* my witnesses." Thus, Jesus' emphasis was on being rather than doing. Our witness must be more than mere talk, it is to be a way of life. Certainly we witness with our words; however, it is also important that we witness with our lives.

Paul wrote the believers in Rome and explained to them how he had lead the Gentiles to obey God by what he had "said and done" (Rom. 15:18). Or, as one translator puts it, "I have won them by my message and by the good way I have lived before them" (TLB). Paul went on to say that he had done this "all by the Holy Spirit's power."

Yesterday, we discussed how the Holy Spirit empowers us to witness with powerful words and mighty works. Today, we will look at how the Spirit enables us to witness with our lives. We will discuss three ways the Spirit works in our lives enabling us to authentically represent Christ to a lost world.

The Spirits Sets Us Apart

The first way the Spirit enables us to authentically represent Christ to the world is *by sanctifying us and making us holy.* Paul wrote that we are "sanctified...by the Spirit of our God" (1 Cor. 6:11). The word, *sanctify,* literally means to consecrate or set apart. Thus, when we come to Christ, the Holy Spirit sets us apart from the world and consecrates us to God and His mission. We are then to live Christ-honoring lives. John wrote, "Whoever claims to live in him must walk as Jesus did" (1 John 2:6).

We must live in holiness because we represent a holy God to a corrupt world. Paul urged the Philippian Christians to live "blameless and pure" lives in the midst of a "warped and crooked generation" (Phil. 2:15). If they would do this, he said, they would "shine like stars" in the night sky (v. 16).

We can live this way only through the Spirit's power. Paul admonished the Galatians, "Live by the Spirit, and you will not gratify the desires of the sinful nature" (Gal. 5:16). The Holy Spirit alone can free us from our self-centeredness to truly serve God and His mission. The Spirit further sanctifies us by giving us the moral courage we need to obey Christ's command to "go and make disciples of all nations" (Matt. 28:19).

The Spirit Creates in Us the Character of Jesus

A second important way the Spirit enables us to authentically represent Christ to the world is *by creating in us the character of Jesus.* People were drawn to Jesus for at least three reasons: His grace-filled words, His powerful works, and His beautiful life.

Concerning His words, the Bible says, "All spoke well of him and were amazed at the gracious words that came from his lips" (Luke 4:22). Concerning His powerful works, John says that "a great crowd of people followed him because they saw the miraculous signs he had performed on the sick" (John 6:2). Concerning His beautiful life, John wrote, "He never sinned, nor ever deceived anyone" (1 John 3:5 NLT).

As we abide in Christ and walk in the Spirit, the Holy Spirit works in us forming us into the image of our Savior. Paul said that we are "transformed into his image with ever-increasing glory, which comes from…the Spirit" (2 Cor. 3:18). This Christ-like image is exhibited in the "fruit of the Spirit." Paul wrote, "The fruit of the Spirit is love, joy, peace, patience, kindness, goodness, faithfulness, gentleness and self-control" (Gal. 5:22-23). Together these fruit give us a glimpse into the character of Jesus. They grow in our lives as we abide in Christ and live our lives "in step with the Spirit" (Gal. 5:25).

The Spirit Fills Us with God's Love

A third important way the Spirit enables us to authentically represent Christ to the world is *by filling our hearts with God's love.* Paul wrote, "God has poured out his love into our hearts by the Holy Spirit, whom he has given us" (Rom. 5:5). As we allow the Spirit to work in our lives, He enables us to love as Jesus loved.

This Spirit-engendered love will inspire us to reach out to those in need. The Bible says that, when Jesus saw people, "He had compassion on them and healed their sick" (Matt. 14:14). One reason Jesus moved with compassion is that the Holy Spirit was working in His life. Peter put it like this, "God anointed Jesus of Nazareth with the Holy Spirit and power, and…he went around doing good and healing all who were under the power of the devil, because God was with him" (Acts 10:38).

Only the Spirit can cause us to love and care for people as Jesus did. We must therefore allow Him to work deeply in our lives rooting out all selfishness and prejudice. Then, when people see the compassion of Christ working in and through us, they will be drawn to Jesus. (We will discuss this subject more in a different context on Day 24.)

Walking with the Holy Spirit

Now that you have concluded today's reading, take a few moments to complete the following exercise.

A Truth to Embrace: The Holy Spirit wants to work in my life to enable me to authentically represent Christ to a lost world.

A Commitment to Make: I will allow the Holy Spirit to work in me producing the character of Jesus in my life.

A Prayer to Pray: "Let the beauty of Jesus be seen in me; all His wonderful passion and purity. O Thou Spirit divine, all my being refine, 'til the beauty of Jesus is seen in me" (from the song "The Beauty of Jesus" by Albert Osborn and Tom Jones).

A Verse to Memorize: "Live by the Spirit, and you will not gratify the desires of the sinful nature." (Gal. 5:16)

Day 15

The Spirit Works in the Lives of Unbelievers

The last few days we have looked at how the Holy Spirit enables Christians to effectively participate in God's missions to redeem the nations. The Spirit, however, not only works in the life of the proclaimer of the gospel, He also works in the lives of those who receive the word. Today, we will look at three ways the Holy Spirit works on and in the lives of nonbelievers preparing them to receive the message of Christ and be saved.

The Spirit Prepares Hearts

The first way that the Holy Spirit works in the lives of unbelievers is by preparing their hearts to receive the message of truth. Jesus said, "No one can come to me unless the Father who sent me draws him" (John 6:44). The Father does His work of drawing people to Christ through the Holy Spirit. This can happen a number of ways.

The Spirit can secretly work in the lives of sinners making them aware of their need for God. He may give someone a dream or a vision, opening his or her heart to the message of Christ. This is what happened to Cornelius in Acts 10. The Spirit gave him a vision of an angel who told him to send for Peter who would tell him what he must do. Even today, the Spirit of God gives certain unsaved individuals dreams or visions of Christ. This work of the Spirit seems to be especially common among Muslim men and women who are sincerely seeking after God.

The Spirit most often works in the lives of nonbelievers as they hear the gospel being proclaimed. He opens their minds to comprehend the truth of what is being said. This very thing happened to a woman named Lydia in the Book of Acts. As Paul talked to her about Christ, "the Lord opened her heart to respond to Paul's message" (Acts 16:4).

The Holy Spirit works in the same way today. When we share Christ with the lost, the Spirit moves on their hearts, enabling them to receive the message. Because of this, we can be confident that, when we go and preach the gospel, the Spirit of the Lord will work with us pointing people to Christ (Mark 16:20).

The Spirit Convicts of Sin

A second way the Holy Spirit works in the lives of unbelievers is by convicting them of their sin. Jesus said, "When the Counsellor [the Holy Spirit] comes, he will convict the world of guilt in regard to sin…" (John 16:8). This is what occurred on the Day of Pentecost. The Holy Spirit was poured out on the waiting disciples. Then Peter stood and proclaimed the gospel to the gathered crowd. As he preached, the Spirit of the Lord moved in the people's hearts making them aware that they were sinners and in need of a Savior. The Bible says, "They were cut to the heart" and cried out, imploring Peter to tell them what they must do to be saved (Acts 2:37).

Paul describes how the Spirit works in the lives of unbelievers when they come into a place where the Spirit of God is moving:

> If an unbeliever…comes in while everybody is prophesying, he will be convinced by all that he is a sinner and will be judged by all, and the secrets of his heart will be laid bare. So he will fall down and worship God, exclaiming, "God is really among you!" (1 Cor. 14:24-25)

This is why it is so important for every believer to remain full of the Holy Spirit. If we will do this, the Holy Spirit will give our words power so that they will penetrate people's hearts. It is also vital that the Spirit of the Lord be present and moving in our church services. His very presence will draw people to Christ.

The Spirit Regenerates Repentant Sinners

A third way the Holy Spirit works in the lives of unbelievers is by regenerating repentant sinners. By this, we mean that, when a sinner comes to Christ and repents of his or her sins, the Holy Spirit makes them into a new person in Christ. Paul put it like this: "If anyone is in Christ, he is a new creation; the old has gone, the new has come!" (2 Cor. 5:17).

Jesus explained to Nicodemus, "No one can see the kingdom of God unless he is born again" (John 3:3). When Nicodemus asked how someone could be born a second time, Jesus replied, "I tell you the truth, no one can enter the kingdom of God unless he is born of water and the Spirit. Flesh gives birth to flesh, but the Spirit gives birth to spirit" (v. 6). Paul explained that we are saved "through the washing of rebirth and renewal by the Holy Spirit" (Titus 3:5).

When a repentant sinner comes to Christ, puts his or her faith in Him alone for salvation, and repents of their sins, a miracle takes place. The Spirit enters the person's life, changes them from the inside out, and makes them new creations in Christ (2 Cor. 5:17).

Has this happened in your life? If not, humble yourself before God, and sincerely pray this prayer:

"Lord Jesus, I believe that you are the Son of God, the Savior of the world. I admit that I am a sinner, and I repent of my sins. I open my heart to you, come into my life and be my Lord and Savior. By your Holy Spirit, make me a new creation in Christ. In your name, I pray. Amen."

Walking with the Holy Spirit

Now that you have concluded today's reading, take a few moments to complete the following exercise.

A Truth to Embrace: When I share Christ with others, I can know that the Holy Spirit is at work in their lives drawing them to Him.

A Commitment to Make: I commit to remain full of the Spirit and faithfully share the message of Christ with my lost family and friends.

A Prayer to Pray: Dear Holy Spirit, work in the lives of my unsaved family and friends drawing them to Christ. And give me the courage and wisdom I need to present Christ to them.

A Verse to Memorize: "No one can come to me unless the Father who sent me draws him." (John 6:44)

Part 5

The Baptism in the Holy Spirit

What Is the Baptism in the Holy Spirit?

A s the Book of Acts begins, Jesus leaves His disciples with a parting command. "Do not leave Jerusalem," He orders them, "but wait for the gift my Father promised…for John baptized with water, but in a few days you will be baptized with the Holy Spirit" (Acts 1:4-5). He then gives them a final promise: "You will receive power when the Holy Spirit comes on you, and you will be my witnesses in Jerusalem, and in all Judea and Samaria, and to the ends of the earth" (Acts 1:8). Finally, Luke tells us, "He was taken up before their very eyes, and a cloud hid him from their sight" (v. 9).

Jesus thus commanded His disciples to wait in Jerusalem until they had been empowered by the Holy Spirit. We talked a bit about this on Day 12. Today, and the next four days, we will expand on the subject. We will discuss the pathway into the Spirit-empowered life, an experience that Jesus, John the Baptist, and Peter all referred to as being "baptized in the Holy Spirit" (Luke 3:16; Acts 1:5; 11:16).

The Experience Defined

What then is this baptism in the Holy Spirit the New Testament talks about? Before we discuss what the experience *is,* let's look briefly at what it *is not.* We do this because some hold sincere but mistaken ideas concerning the experience.

What the baptism in the Holy Spirit is not. First, the baptism in the Holy Spirit is not salvation. We know this because Jesus' disciples were already saved when Jesus commanded them to stay in Jerusalem to receive the gift of the Holy Spirit. Secondly, the baptism in the Holy Spirit is not "entire sanctification." We know this because Jesus had already cleansed His disciples before the Day of Pentecost (John 15:3). Finally, the baptism in the Holy Spirit is not a "second blessing" that Christ gives to His followers. It is rather a divine empowering that He gives them to enable them to effectively participate in His mission to redeem the nations. Let's discuss this idea a bit further.

What the baptism in the Holy Spirit is. Scripture describes Spirit baptism at least three important ways. First, Scripture presents Spirit baptism as a powerful *life-transforming experience from God.* Jesus once depicted the experience as a clothing with "power from on high" (Luke 24:49). The transforming effect of Spirit baptism is demonstrated in the story of Peter. Before Pentecost, he was timid and fearful (Mark 14:69-72). However, after he was baptized in the Holy Spirit, he became a bold witness for Christ (Acts 2:14-39).

Peter was transformed from the inside out. The same thing happens today. When someone is baptized in the Holy Spirit, his or her life is dramatically altered. The Holy Spirit fills them and gives them the inner strength they need to become powerful witnesses for Christ and His kingdom.

Second, the baptism in the Holy Spirit is a *promise for all believers.* Jesus called the experience "the promise of the Father" (Luke 24:49; Acts 1:4). On the Day of Pentecost, Peter announced to the crowd, "The promise is for you and your children and for all who are far off—for all whom the Lord our God will call" (Acts 2:38-39). This means that, even today, some two thousand years later, we too can claim this wonderful promise from God. Jesus promised, "Everyone who asks receives" (Luke 11:9). He then added, "The Father in heaven [will] give the Holy Spirit to those who ask him!" (v. 13).

Finally, it is important to understand that the baptism in the Holy Spirit is a *command from God.* The experience is so essential to the Christian life that the Bible does not present it as an option. Jesus commanded His disciples to "wait for the gift my Father promised... For John baptized with water, but in a few days you will be baptized with the Holy Spirit" (Acts 1:4-5).

The Experience Exhibited

Having briefly defined Spirit baptism, let's now look at how in Scripture it is exhibited in people's lives. The importance of the experience is demonstrated in the life of Jesus and in the practice of the early church as recorded in the Book of Acts. Jesus himself did not begin His ministry until He was first empowered by the Holy Spirit (Luke 3:21-13). The same was true for the apostles. They did not begin their ministries until they were empowered by the Spirit (Acts 2).

This *empowerment-results-in-witness pattern* continued through the Book of Acts. For instance, when Paul received the Spirit, he "at once he began to preach in the synagogues that Jesus is the Son of God" (Acts 9:20). In Ephesus, the Holy Spirit came on the disciples, and "they spoke in tongues and prophesied" (Acts 19:6). They then began to proclaim the gospel so effectively that "all the Jews and Greeks who lived in the province of Asia heard the word of the Lord" (v. 10).

Luke repeats this *empowerment-results-in-witness pattern* throughout Acts to show the importance of every follower of Jesus being baptized in the Holy Spirit. Today, if we are to effectively continue the ministry of Jesus and the apostles, every member of the church must follow their example and be baptized in the Holy Spirit just as they were.

The Experience Explained

The New Testament uses three word pictures to describe the experience of being baptized in the Holy Spirit. Those three word pictures are believers are "baptized in" the Holy Spirit (Luke 3:16; Acts 1:5; 11:16); the Holy Spirit "comes upon" believers (Acts 1:8; 10:44; 19:6); and believers are "filled with" the Holy Spirit (Acts 2:14; 4:31; Eph. 5:18). Each of these word pictures tells us something important about the experience:

1. Baptized in. First, Jesus depicted the experience as a "baptism in" the Holy Spirit. To baptize something means to submerge, or plunge, it into water or some other liquid. This is what happens when a minister baptizes a new believer. He plunges them into the water until they are completely submerged. In the same way, when a believer is baptized in the Holy Spirit, Jesus takes them and plunges them into the Holy Spirit. As a result, they are covered with and overwhelmed by God's power and presence. Spirit baptism is truly a powerful, life-changing experience.

2, Coming upon. Second, Scripture pictures the baptism in the Holy Spirit as the Holy Spirit "coming upon" believers. Jesus told His disciples, "You will receive power when the Holy Spirit *comes on you*..." (Acts 1:8). You will remember that, on the Day of Pentecost, tongues of fire *"came to rest* on each of them" (2:3). This pattern of the Holy Spirit coming upon believers continues throughout the Book of Acts. For instance, in Ephesus, "when Paul placed his hands on [the twelve disciples], the Holy Spirit *came on* them..." (19:6). In Acts, every time the Holy Spirit comes upon someone the result is Spirit-empowered witness in word and deed. We can expect the same to happen today.

3. Filled with. Finally, the Bible depicts the baptism in the Holy Spirit as a "filling with" the Holy Spirit. On the Day of Pentecost, "all of them were filled with the Holy Spirit and began to speak in other tongues as the Spirit enabled them" (Acts 2:4). The term "filled with" is used several other times in Acts (4:8, 31; 9:17; 13:9, 52). The same moment a man or woman is baptized in the Holy Spirit, they are also filled with the Spirit. The Spirit of God comes into them saturating every part of their being. In Acts, every time the author uses this term, the result is Spirit-empowered speech.

Walking with the Holy Spirit

Now that you have concluded today's reading, take a few moments to complete the following exercise.

A Truth to Embrace: I understand that Spirit baptism is a powerful, life-altering experience, and that Jesus has commanded every disciple to be baptized in the Holy Spirit.

A Commitment to Make: I commit to seek the Spirit's empowerment, and then to endeavor to walk daily in the Spirit's power.

A Prayer to Pray: Dear Jesus, pour out Your Spirit on me and fill and empower me to effectively represent You to a needy world.

A Verse to Memorize: "Do not get drunk on wine, which leads to debauchery. Instead, be filled with the Spirit." (Eph. 5:18)

Why Must Every Christian Be Baptized in the Holy Spirit?

T he wise leader not only tells people what they must do; he or she explains to them why their task is important and how it fits into the big picture of things. This is what Jesus did. When He commanded His disciples to be baptized in the Holy Spirit, He explained to them the big picture, and He told them exactly why they needed the experience. He said to them, "In a few days you will be baptized with the Holy Spirit" (Acts 1:5). He then explained, "You will receive power when the Holy Spirit comes on you; and you will be my witnesses in Jerusalem, and in all Judea and Samaria, and to the ends of the earth" (v. 8).

Today we will look at the big picture. We will answer two important questions: "Why did Jesus command His disciples to be baptized in the Holy Spirit?" and "Why is it so important for every Christian to receive this experience today?" In answering these questions, we will first restate the primary reason every Christian must all be filled with the Spirit. Then, we will look at four other important reasons we must allbe filled with the Spirit. We will further note how each of these secondary reasons relates to the primary reason.

Power to Witness

As we have already discussed, the primary reason every follower of Jesus must be baptized in the Holy Spirit is so that he or she may be empowered as Christ's witness to the lost (Acts 1:8). The Master has ordered each of us to "Go out to the roads and country lanes and make them come in, so that my house will be full" (Luke 14:23). He further commands us to "Go into all the world and preach the good news to all creation" (Mark 16:15). We can do this only through the Spirit's power.

It is important, however, to understand that our witness to the world involves more than just our words. It involves every aspect of our lives. With this in mind, let's look at four other reasons every Christ-follower must be empowered by the Holy Spirit, and how each of those reasons relates to our witness to a lost world.

Power to Live for Christ

The second reason every Christian must be baptized in the Holy Spirit is that the Holy Spirit gives us the ability to live Christ-honoring lives. We discussed this on Day 14; however, it bears repeating here. With the baptism in the Holy Spirit comes greater power to live in true holiness and in selfless concern for others. Our holy God commands us to be holy that we may shine as lights in a dark world (Phil. 2:15)

On our own, we could never do this. However, the Spirit's empowering enables us to overcome temptation and live in dignity before God and man. God promises, "I will put my Spirit in you and

94

move you to follow my decrees and be careful to keep my laws" (Ezek. 36:27).

Power to Pray More Effectively

Another reason every believer needs to be filled with the Spirit is because, in the words of Paul, "We do not know how to pray as we should" (Rom. 8:26, NASB). Our best efforts at prayer are woefully inadequate. Paul however continues, "The Spirit helps our weakness." He does this by filling us and praying through us "with groans that words cannot express." Such prayer includes Spirit-inspired prayer in tongues. What's more, on such occassions "the Spirit intercedes for the saints in accordance with God's will" (v. 27). Paul referred to this kind of prayer as "prayer in the Spirit" (1 Cor. 14:15).

Such Spirit-directed prayer is an essential element of effective witness. Someone has rightly said that the army of God is never so tall as when it marches on its knees. And prayer is never so powerful as when it is energized by the Holy Spirit.

Power to Love

A fourth reason every Christian must be baptized in the Holy Spirit is because with the Spirit's infilling comes a deeper and more active love for God. Paul wrote, "God has poured out his love into our hearts by the Holy Spirit, whom he has given us" (Rom. 5: 5). He also wrote that "the fruit of the Spirit is love" (Gal. 5:22). Thus, when we are filled with the Spirit, and learn to walk daily with the Spirit, we come to know Christ more intimately and love Him more deeply.

The night before Jesus' crucifixion, He met with His disciples in an upper room. There, He told them, "I will not leave you as orphans; I will come to you" (John 14:18). Jesus was promising to send the Holy Spirit whom, He said, would come to take His place (v. 16). On that same evening, Jesus told His disciples to "remain in my love" (15:9). The context of this statement shows that we remain in Christ's love by living in relationship with the Holy Spirit. As we thus live in the Spirit, we experience a deeper relationship with Christ.

The Holy Spirit will also create in our hearts a deeper love for those for whom Christ died. Jesus said that God loved the world so much that He gave His only Son to die for their sins (John 3:16). If we will allow Him, the Holy Spirit will create that same love for the lost in our hearts.

Power to Do the Works of Christ

A fifth and final reason every follower of Jesus must be baptized in the Holy Spirit is that with Spirit baptism comes power to do the works of Christ. Jesus promised, "I tell you the truth, anyone who has faith in me will do what I have been doing. He will do even greater things than these, because I am going to the Father" (John 14:12). He then explained how this would happen. When He arrived at the Father's throne, He said, "I will ask the Father and he will give you another Counselor to be with you forever—the Spirit of truth" (John 14:16-17). Jesus is saying that we can do the same works He did because we can be empowered by the same Holy Spirit who empowered Him to fulfill His ministry (Luke 4:18-19; Acts 10:38).

Being full of the Spirit thus enables us to replicate Jesus' works in our ministries. These works of Jesus include powerful proclamation of the gospel, life transformative teaching, and miraculous signs and wonders. They demonstrate to the world that the message of the gospel is true and that the kingdom of God has come. For these and other compelling reasons, every disciple of Jesus must be filled with, and remain full of, the Holy Spirit.

Walking with the Holy Spirit

Now that you have concluded today's reading, take a few moments to complete the following exercise.

A Truth to Embrace: If I am to live in close relationship with Christ, and effectively represent Him to a lost world, I must be filled with the Holy Spirit.

A Commitment to Make: I will be empowered by the Holy Spirit so that I can more effectively serve Christ and reach out to the lost with His love.

A Prayer to Pray: Holy Spirit, fill me again and give me Christ's love and compassion for lost and hurting people.

A Verse to Memorize: "God has poured out his love into our hearts by the Holy Spirit, whom he has given us." (Rom. 5:5)

You Can Know You Have Been Filled

After the Day of Pentecost, the church grew rapidly. Soon the twelve apostles became overburdened with administrative matters. They needed someone to relieve them of this duty so they could devote themselves to prayer and proclamation of the word. So, they asked the church to choose seven men from among them who were "known to be full of the Spirit and wisdom" (Acts 6:3). They would then appoint them over this duty.

This then begs the question, how can one determine if he or she has been filled with the Holy Spirit? What distinguishes them from others who have not been filled? Or to personalize the question, "How can I know for certain that I have been baptized in the Holy Spirit according to the biblical pattern?"

The good news is that one does not have to wonder whether he or she has been filled with the Holy Spirit. The New Testament presents a number of indicators of the Spirit-empowered life. The Book of Acts, however, focuses on two primary signs, Spirit-inspired tongues and Spirit-empowered witness. Let's look more closely at these two signs.

Spirit-Inspired Tongues

In Acts, when people were initially baptized in the Holy Spirit, they miraculously spoke in tongues as the Holy Spirit gave them the ability. This first happened on the Day of Pentecost: "All of them were filled with the Holy Spirit and began to speak in other tongues as the Spirit enabled them" (Acts 2:4). Speaking in tongues happened two more times in the Book of Acts. It occurred a few months later in the coastal city of Caesarea. On that occasion, as Peter was preaching, "the Holy Spirit came on all who heard the message." The Jewish believers with Peter were convinced that these Gentiles had received the Spirit, "for they heard them speaking in tongues and praising God" (10:44-46).

Twenty-five years later, Paul arrived in the city of Ephesus. There he encountered twelve disciples. After a brief conversation with them, "Paul placed his hands on them, the Holy Spirit came on them, and they spoke in tongues and prophesied" (19:6). Note how, in each of these instances, when believers were baptized in the Holy Spirit, they spoke in tongues.

On the two other occasions in Acts when people were initially baptized in the Spirit, the context implies that they too spoke in tongues. The first instance occurred in the city of Samaria in Acts 8. When Peter and John laid hands on the new Christians there, something extraordinary happened. It was so remarkable that Simon the sorcerer wanted to purchase the ability to lay hands on people to receive the Holy Spirit. Scholars, both Pentecostal and non-Pentecostal, believe that Simon likely saw these new believers speaking in tongues.

On yet another occasion, in Acts 9, Ananias laid hands on Saul of Tarsus, and the apostle-to-be received the Holy Spirit (v. 17). Although the text does not say that he, at that moment, spoke in tongues, Paul later testified, "I thank God that I speak in tongues more than all of you" (1 Cor. 14:18). The most likely time for him to have begun speaking in tongues was the moment he was baptized in the Holy Spirit, as did others in Acts.

Scholars call this kind of speaking in tongues the "initial physical evidence" of one's being baptized in the Holy Spirit. It could also be called the "normative missional sign" that one has been empowered to witness for Christ. In other words, when someone is baptized in the Holy Spirit, God will cause them to speak in tongues as a sign that He has empowered them as Christ's witnesses to the lost.

Spirit-Empowered Witness

In Acts, another consistent result of believers being filled with the Holy Spirit is that they immediately began to witness with power. Peter is a good example of this. A careful reading of the Pentecost story reveals that, on that day, Peter spoke by the Spirit two times. First, along with the 120 or so other disciples, he spoke in tongues "as the Spirit enabled them" (2:4). Then, he spoke by the Spirit a second time. This time, however, Peter spoke in the common language. He preached the gospel in the power of the Spirit, thus fulfilling Jesus' promise in Acts 1:8: "But you will receive power when the Holy Spirit comes on you; and you will be my witnesses…" This pattern is repeated throughout Acts. When people are filled with the Spirit, they quickly begin to witness for Christ.

For example, in Acts 4, Peter was again filled with the Spirit, this time in the presence of the Jewish authorities. He then boldly announced, "Salvation is found in no one else, for there is no other name under heaven [other than the name of Jesus]...by which we must be saved" (Acts 4:8-12). Later, when God again poured out His Spirit on the church in Jerusalem, they "spoke the word of God boldly" (4:31). Again, when Paul first received the Holy Spirit, he "at once began to preach in the synagogues that Jesus is the Son of God" (9:20). In Acts, every time someone is filled with the Spirit they begin to witness for Jesus.

All of this to say that one can know that he or she has been baptized in the Holy Spirit when they begin to speak in tongues, as believers did in the Book of Acts. They should also expect to be filled with the passion and power to more effectively share Christ with others. Both of these signs are clear indications that one has been truly empowered by the Spirit.

Walking with the Holy Spirit

Now that you have concluded today's reading, take a few moments to complete the following exercise.

A Truth to Embrace: I can know that I have been baptized in the Holy Spirit when I speak in tongues and receive passion and power to witness for Christ.

A Commitment to Make: I commit myself to be filled with the Spirit like the disciples on the Day of Pentecost, with the accompanying signs of speaking in tongues and bold witness.

A Prayer to Pray: Jesus, I commit myself to You and to Your mission. Come, Holy Spirit, fill me now, and empower me to speak for Christ.

A Verse to Memorize: "All of them were filled with the Holy Spirit and began to speak in other tongues as the Spirit enabled them." (Acts 2:4)

Day 18: You Can Know You Have Been Filled

Day 19

You Can Receive the Holy Spirit Today

We now come to one of the most important lessons in our study. In it we will address the issue of receiving the Holy Spirit. For what is the value of our understanding the meaning and importance of Spirit baptism if we do not personally experience it?

We will thus consider three matters related to receiving the Holy Spirit. First, we will talk about what one must know before he or she approaches Christ to ask Him to fill them with the Spirit. Then, we will discuss how one may actually receive the Holy Spirit by faith. Finally, we will address the related issue of speaking in tongues.

Before You Ask

Before one asks God to fill him or her with the Holy Spirit, it is important to understand three important spiritual truths.

1. Be born again. First, the seeker must know that before he or she can be filled with the Spirit, they must be truly born again. Jesus said, "No one can see the kingdom of God unless he is born again"

(John 3:3). Then later, speaking about those who do not know God, Jesus said, "The world cannot receive [the Holy Spirit], because it neither sees him nor knows him" (14:17). Consequently, before being filled with the Spirit, one must first receive Jesus Christ as his or her Lord and Savior. They can do this by repenting of their sins and fully trusting in Christ for salvation. They will then be candidates for the Spirit's empowering.

2. Hunger and thirst after God. Secondly, in preparation for receiving the Holy Spirit, one must hunger for the things God. Jesus promised, "Blessed are those who hunger and thirst for righteousness, for they will be filled" (Matt. 5:6). On another occasion, He cried out, saying, "If anyone is thirsty, let him come to me and drink. Whoever believes in me, as the Scripture has said, streams of living water will flow from within him" (John 7:37-38). Jesus was speaking about receiving the Spirit. He was saying that He will happily give His Spirit to anyone who is thirsty for more of God.

3. Be ready to witness. Third, to receive the Spirit, one must be prepared to obey God and become His witness. Peter declared that God gives the Holy Spirit "to those who obey Him" (Acts 5:32). He was talking specifically about obeying Christ's command to be His witness (vv. 28-29). In other words, if one is prepared to witness for Christ, God is prepared to give him or her His Holy Spirit.

Receive by Faith

Let's now talk about how we may receive the promise of the Spirit as our own. Jesus has given us clear instructions. He said,

> So I say to you: "Ask and it will be given to you; seek and you will find; knock and the door will be opened to you. For everyone who asks receives; he who seeks finds; and to him who knocks, the door will be opened. Which of you fathers, if your son asks

for a fish, will give him a snake instead? Or if he asks for an egg, will give him a scorpion? If you then, though you are evil, know how to give good gifts to your children, how much more will your Father in heaven give the Holy Spirit to those who ask him!" (Luke 11:9-13)

To the question, "How can one receive the gift of the Holy Spirit?" Jesus answers, you receive by simply asking in faith (Luke 11:13). Paul told the Galatians, "By faith we…receive the promise of the Spirit" (Gal. 3:14). God will freely give the Holy Spirit to those who sincerely and believingly ask.

Any faithful follower of Jesus can receive the Holy Spirit by taking three simple "steps of faith":

Step 1: Ask in faith. First, Jesus taught that we must ask in faith (Luke 11:9, 13). We must simply and sincerely present our request to God, believing that He will hear and answer our prayer. Remember, God is more eager to give you the Spirit than you are to receive it. With this in mind, sincerely and confidently pray this prayer:

Lord, I believe your promise. I believe that if I ask for the Spirit, you will give me the Spirit. So right now, in Jesus' name, I ask you, give me the Holy Spirit, and empower me as your witness.

As you pray, believe that God is hearing and answering your prayer. Believe that, at this very moment, He is giving you the Holy Spirit. As you do, you will begin to sense the Spirit's presence as He comes upon you.

Step 2: Receive by faith. Second, Jesus taught that we must receive the Spirit by faith (Luke 11:10). Receiving the Spirit is a bold, present-tense step of faith. It occurs the moment the promise is fully believed and boldly acted upon. Remember Jesus' words: "Whatever you ask in prayer, believe that you have received it, and it will be yours" (Mark 11:24). Pray this simple prayer, *Holy Spirit, come inside me, and fill me.* Now, believe that you have received. Sense the Spirit's Presence deep inside you—in your innermost being. Once you have sensed the Spirit's presence within, it is time to take the third step.

Step 3: Speak in faith. Like the 120 disciples on the Day of Pentecost, you should now speak out in faith as the Holy Spirit gives utterance. The Bible says, "All of them were filled with the Holy Spirit and began to speak in other tongues as the Spirit enabled them" (Acts 2:4). You can do the same. Once you sense the Spirit's presence deep inside, allow Him to gush forth from your "innermost being." As He does, cooperate with what He is doing. Yield to Him your vocal organs and lips. You will begin to speak words in a language you have never learned. When this happens, do not be afraid. God is empowering you to be His Spirit-empowered witness.

This act of faith can be compared to Peter's step of faith when, at the word of Jesus, he stepped from the boat and began to walk on water. His bold step of faith resulted in a miracle—and so will yours! (Mark 14:28-29).

Once you begin to speak, yield yourself more and more to the Spirit. Let the words flow. Continue to speak, holding nothing back, fully trusting God to do His part. Praise the Lord! You have been baptized in the Holy Spirit, and you have been empowered as Christ's Spirit-inspired spokesperson.

Speaking in Tongues

It may be helpful to say a bit more about speaking in tongues, since this is often a new and perhaps strange phenomenon to those who have never experienced it. It is important to understand that, when you speak in tongues, the words you speak will not come from your mind, as in natural speech. They will come from deep inside, from your spirit. Jesus said, "He who believes in Me, as the Scripture said, 'From his innermost being will flow rivers of living water'" (John 7:38, NASB). Paul said that the "one who speaks in a tongue does not speak to men but to God; for no one understands, but in [or "with"] his spirit he speaks mysteries" (1 Cor. 14:2). Paul stated further, "If I pray in a language I don't understand, my spirit is praying, but I don't know what I am saying" (v. 14).

Remember, your speaking will not be forced. It will be a natural flow of supernatural words. You should simply allow it to happen, and cooperate fully with the Spirit by boldly speaking out in faith. (We will talk more about speaking in tongues on Day 26.)

Walking with the Holy Spirit

Now that you have concluded today's reading, take a few moments to complete the following exercise.

A Truth to Embrace: I can receive the Holy Spirit today by simply asking, receiving, and speaking in faith.

A Commitment to Make: I commit myself to seek and be filled with the Holy Spirit as were the disciples in the Book of Acts.

A Prayer to Pray: Dear Holy Spirit, come upon me now, fill me, and enable me to speak in faith as the Spirit gives utterance.

A Verse to Memorize: "If you then, though you are evil, know how to give good gifts to your children, how much more will your Father in heaven give the Holy Spirit to those who ask him!" (Luke 11:13)

Day 20

You Can Help Others Receive the Holy Spirit

When the apostles in Jerusalem heard that the Samaritans were being saved, they immediately send Peter and John to pray with them that they might receive the Holy Spirit (Acts 8:14-17). As did Jesus, the apostles placed great emphasis on all believers being baptized in the Holy Spirit. They did this because they fully grasped the significance of Jesus' parting words to the church, when He told them, "You will receive power when the Holy Spirit comes on you; and you will be my witnesses…to the ends of the earth" (Acts 1:8). They knew that if the gospel was to advance to the ends of the earth, every follower of Jesus must be empowered by the Holy Spirit. Only then would they be able to effectively witness for Christ.

This truth remains until today. If our churches are to rapidly advance and the lost are to be won to Christ, we too must work to ensure that every member of the church is empowered by the Holy Spirit. Yesterday, we discussed how one can be filled with the Spirit. Today, we will discuss how we can lead others into the experience.

Preparing Believers to Receive the Spirit

To lead believers into the baptism in the Holy Spirit we must first prepare them to receive. We can do this in three ways: by creating a desire in their hearts for the Spirit-empowered life, by helping them to better understand the experience, and by building their faith in preparation for receiving the Spirit. Let's look closer at each of these ways.

1. Create desire. We can create desire in people's hearts to receive the Spirit by showing them the benefits of living the Spirit-filled life. These benefits include power to witness, a closer relationship with Christ, assistance in prayer, and much more, as we have discussed in this study. As new believers observe these spiritual dynamics being lived out in the lives of Spirit-filled Christians, a desire is birthed in their hearts for a closer walk with the Spirit.

We can further create a desire in people's lives by cultivating the Spirit's presence in our church services. When people encounter the Spirit in church, He creates a desire in their hearts to know Him better.

2. Help to understand. Next, we can prepare people to receive the Spirit by helping them to better understand the purpose and nature of the experience. We do this by preaching and teaching often on the subject. As individuals become more knowledgeable, they are better prepared to respond to the Spirit.

3. Build faith. Finally, we can prepare people to receive the Spirit by building their faith. Paul states that "by faith we...receive the promise of the Spirit" (Gal. 3:14). We build people's faith by sharing with them Christ's promise to give the Holy Spirit to "everyone who asks" (Luke 11:10). Other promises we may want to share with them are found in Mark 11:24 and Acts 2:39. We must also give people many opportunities to receive the Spirit. Prayer for the Spirit must become a regular event in our worship gatherings.

Praying with Believers to Receive the Spirit

When praying with someone to receive the Spirit, it is often helpful to lead them in two prayers.

The prayer of asking. First, lead the seeker in asking for the Spirit. Remember, Jesus' promise: "Ask and it will be given to you" (Luke 11:9). Much as you would lead a sinner in the sinner's prayer, you can lead the new believer in a prayer asking to be filled with the Spirit. The prayer may proceed as follows, with the candidate repeating each line:

Lord, I come now to be filled with the Holy Spirit... You promised that I would receive power when the Spirit came upon me... I need that power to be your witness... You also promised that everyone who asks receives... I am asking; therefore, I expect to receive... When I receive I will speak in faith... I will not be afraid... I will begin to pray in tongues as Your Spirit gives me utterance.

After you have prayed, assure the candidate that God has heard their prayer, and that He is ready now to fill them with the Holy Spirit. Encourage the candidate to be spiritually sensitive to the Spirit's working. You may want to take a few moments to worship the Lord together, responding to the Spirit's presence.

The step of faith. After you have lead the seeker in asking for the Spirit, and you have taken a few moments to sense the Spirit's presence, lead the seeker in his or her step of faith (see Mark 11:24). You will remember that yesterday we compared receiving the Spirit to Peter's step of faith when he obeyed Jesus' command, stepped out of the boat, and began to walk on water. To lead the seeker in their step of faith, ask them to lift their hands toward heaven and, in faith, pray this simple prayer: *Lord, right now, in Jesus Name, I receive the Holy Spirit.* This prayer provides a definite point where the seeker can exercise his or her faith to receive the Holy Spirit. They should, at that moment, *believe that they have received!* The instant the seeker believes, the Spirit will come and fill them. Instruct them to sense Spirit's presence deep inside.

Now, encourage the candidate to act in bold faith and begin to speak, not from their mind, but from deep within, from where he or she senses God's Spirit inside. As he or she yields to the Spirit flowing into and through their being, they will begin to speak words they do not understand. Encourage them not to be fearful but to cooperate fully with the Spirit by continuing to speak in faith.

Counselling Those Who Have Prayed

It is important that after-prayer counseling be given to the candidates. If they have been filled with the Spirit, you will give one kind of counsel; if they have not been filled, you will give another kind.

If the candidate is filled. If the candidate is filled with the Spirit and speaks in tongues, the following advice is appropriate. Tell them that receiving the Spirit is not an end in itself; it is a means to a greater end. The purpose for receiving the Spirit is that we may receive power for life and witness. You may want to say,

> *This is not the end; it's just the beginning. God will now begin to use you in new and powerful ways. Expect to have new power in your life. Go out right now and tell someone about Jesus.*

You may want to add,

You should also spend time each day praying in the Spirit, that is, in tongues. This will give you strength and will remind you of the Spirit's presence in your life.

If the candidate is not filled. If the candidate is not filled with the Spirit at this time, tell them to not be discouraged, and assure them that the promise of Jesus is still true: "Ask and it will be given to you" (Luke 11:9). Tell them that they should keep asking, seeking, and knocking, as Jesus taught. As they do, they should keep in mind Jesus' promise: "Everyone who asks receives" (v. 10). You may want to ask the seeker if he or she wants to pray again. If they do, repeat the above procedure, encouraging them to act in bold faith.

Walking with the Holy Spirit

Now that you have concluded today's reading, take a few moments to complete the following exercise.

A Truth to Embrace: With God's help I can lead others into the baptism in the Holy Spirit.

A Commitment to Make: I will allow God to use me to lead others into the experience of Spirit baptism.

A Prayer to Pray: Dear Holy Spirit, fill me and use me to lead others into the Spirit-empowered life.

A Verse to Memorize: "Then Ananias went to the house and entered it. Placing his hands on Saul, he said, 'Brother Saul, the Lord—Jesus, who appeared to you on the road as you were coming here—has sent me so that you may regain your sight and be filled with the Holy Spirit.'" (Acts 9:17)

Part 6

The Spirit Helps Us

Day 21

The Spirit Helps Us Pray

I f someone were to ask you, "Do you know how to pray?" how would you answer? Most of us would answer in the affirmative. However, we might quickly add, "I need to learn to pray better." This must have been how Jesus' disciples felt when they approached Him and asked, "Lord, teach us to pray, just as John taught his disciples" (Luke 11:1).

Jesus responded to His disciples' request in two ways. First, He gave them a model prayer. Today, we call this prayer the Lord's Prayer. Then, Jesus explained to them how to be filled with the Holy Spirit (vv. 9-13). He was, in effect, saying to them, "If you want to pray like Me, then like Me, you must be filled with the Holy Spirit."

Today, we will examine the intimate relationship between prayer and the Holy Spirit. In doing this, we will discover two important spiritual truths. The first truth is, to be filled with the Holy Spirit, we must pray. The second truth is, to pray, we must be filled with the Holy Spirit. Let's look a bit closer at each of these corresponding spiritual truths.

To Be Filled, We Must Pray

The Bible closely connects receiving the Spirit with prayer. Luke especially emphasizes this relationship. Throughout his gospel and Acts, he consistently associates prayer with the coming of the Spirit. For instance, Luke tells us that Jesus was praying when the Holy Spirit descended upon Him (Luke 3:21-22). Then in Acts, he tells us that before the outpouring of the Spirit at Pentecost, the disciples "all joined together constantly in prayer" (Acts 1:14). Later, they prayed again, and "they were all filled with the Holy Spirit and spoke the word of God boldly" (4:31). Then, in chapters 9 and 10, Luke tells us that Paul was in prayer before He received the Holy Spirit (9:11), and both Cornelius and Peter were in prayer before the Spirit was poured out on the Gentiles in Caesarea (10:2, 9).

This connection between prayer and receiving the Spirit is consistent with Jesus' promise in Luke 11: "So I say to you: Ask [in prayer] and it will be given to you; seek and you will find; knock and the door will be opened to you... your Father in heaven [will] give the Holy Spirit to those who ask him!" (vv. 9-13). In other words, God bestows His Holy Spirit on His children in answer to believing prayer.

We thus learn two important lessons about the relationship between prayer and the experience of the Spirit. First, we learn that, if we want to be filled with the Holy Spirit—or if we want to lead others into the experience—we must pray. Second, we learn that, if we ourselves are to remain full of the Holy Spirit, we must, in the words of Jesus, "Keep on asking... Keep on seeking, and... Keep on knocking" (Luke 11:9, NLT). Or, as Paul tells us, we must "never stop praying" (1 Thess. 5:17, NLT). Just as Jesus lived in constant communion with His Heavenly Father, so must we. Such communion is key to living the Spirit-empowered life.

To Pray, We Must Be Filled

Not only does Scripture teach that to be filled with the Holy Spirit we must pray, it also teaches that, to pray as we should, we must be filled with the Holy Spirit. Paul explained how the Spirit enables our prayer:

> The Spirit helps us in our weakness. We do not know what we ought to pray for, but the Spirit himself intercedes for us with groans that words cannot express. And he who searches our hearts knows the mind of the Spirit, because the Spirit intercedes for the saints in accordance with God's will. (Rom. 8:26-27)

Such prayer in the Spirit can occur in two ways. In general, any prayer that is prompted and directed by the Spirit of God is prayer in the Spirit. Such prayer can be described as a "team effort" between the Spirit himself and the Spirit-filled intercessor. The Holy Spirit prompts and directs the prayer; the intercessor yields and cooperates. However, in Romans 8 when Paul speaks of "groans that words cannot express," he is more specifically speaking of prayer in tongues. He explained this to the Corinthians, where he said, "If I pray in a tongue, my spirit prays" (1 Cor. 14:14).

Oh, how we need this kind of help in prayer. How many urgent needs do we fail to pray for simply because we are unaware of them? Even when we do know what to pray for, we sometimes do not know how to pray because we do not know God's will in the matter. And all too often we pray with the wrong motives, or even worse, we simply lack any motivation to pray at all. At such times, we need the Holy Spirit to come to our aid. As we yield ourselves to the Spirit, He prays through us in words that He gives.

A closer look at Romans 8:26-27 reveals four powerful ways the Spirit helps us in prayer.

1. The Spirit "makes intercession for us." As we, in faith, yield ourselves to the Spirit, He comes to us, fills us with His power and presence, and prays through us directing our prayers.

2. The Spirit prays "with groans which words cannot express." In other words, the Spirit of God prays through us in profound words and phrases that He inspires, that is, in expressions of His own creation.

3. The Spirit "searches our hearts." As we yield to the Spirit's sanctifying power, He purifies our hearts and makes us clean (Psa. 51:10-12). He thus places us in a position where God can answer our prayers (Isa. 59:1).

4. The Spirit "intercedes for the saints according to the will of God." As we allow the Holy Spirit to pray through us, we do so according to God's perfect will. Such prayers have great spiritual power (1 John 5:14-15). Oh, how foolish we would be to neglect the marvelous privilege of prayer in the Spirit.

Walking with the Holy Spirit

Now that you have concluded today's reading, take a few moments to complete the following exercise.

A Truth to Embrace: When I don't know how to pray as I should, the Holy Spirit will come and pray through me.

A Commitment to Make: I commit myself to pray often in the Spirit.

A Prayer to Pray: Holy Spirit, I yield myself to You. Come now, and pray through me "with groans that words cannot express."

Day 21: The Spirit Helps Us Pray

A Verse to Memorize: "In the same way, the Spirit helps us in our weakness. We do not know what we ought to pray for, but the Spirit himself intercedes for us with groans that words cannot express." (Rom. 8:26)

Day 22

The Spirit Enables Our Worship

When Moses was building the Tabernacle in the wilderness, God told him, "Make this tabernacle and all its furnishings exactly like the pattern I will show you" (Exod. 25:9). The Tabernacle was to be the place where Israel would meet and worship God. God therefore demanded that they conduct their worship in a manner He approved.

One of the most important things a Christian can do is to worship God. Since this is true, it must also be true that our worship should be done in a manner that God chooses. Today we will discuss how God wants us to worship Him and how the Holy Spirit helps us to do that.

Worship in Spirit and Truth

Jesus once met a woman at a well. He told her that the time had arrived when "true worshipers will worship the Father in spirit and truth" (John 4:23). He then added, "These are the kind of worshipers the Father seeks." Jesus was saying that, since God is spiritual, those who worship Him must do so in the Spirit, and since He is absolute Truth, those who worship Him must do so in truth. In other words, we must worship God according to the pattern He set down in Scripture.

To worship God in Spirit and in truth involves our human spirits reaching out to God in faith and adoration. True worship is not a matter of dead ritual. It is rather based on a living relationship between a man or woman of God and their Creator. Further, true worship is inspired by the Spirit of God. Paul reminded the Philippian believers that we "worship by the Spirit of God" (Phil. 3:3). We must always allow the Spirit to empower and direct our worship.

Spirit Enabled Worship

How then does the Holy Spirit enable us to truly worship God? He does this by first bringing us into a loving relationship with our heavenly Father. It is out of this relationship that true worship occurs. The Spirit moves in our hearts, fills us with God's love, and prompts us to cry out, "Abba, Father" (Rom. 5:5; 8:15-16). Such a response is to be expected, for Jesus once told His disciples, when the Spirit comes "He will bring glory to me" (John 16:13-14).

Throughout Scripture, the Holy Spirit inspired people to sing and shout praises to God. When the Holy Spirit caused Mary to conceive the Christ child, He also inspired her and her aunt Elizabeth to exult in the Lord (Luke 1:34-55). Later, He did the same thing with Zachariah when John the Baptist was born (67-79). The Spirit also inspired the churches in Corinth and Philippi to worship God (1 Cor. 14:16-17; 25-26; Phil. 3:3).

Once the Spirit even moved Jesus to praise God. On that occasion, the Holy Spirit filled Jesus with such joy that He began to spontaneously glorify His Heavenly Father (Luke 10:21). The same is true today. Those who have learned to yield themselves to the Spirit of the Lord have discovered a glorious freedom in expressing their worship to God (2 Cor. 3:17).

The True Worship Leader

How do these truths apply to our times of congregational worship today? How can we better worship our Lord in Spirit and in truth? We can begin acknowledging Holy Spirit as the true Worship Leader. While we often appoint certain talented individuals to lead the congregation in praise and worship, we must always be very careful to allow the Holy Spirit to remain in charge of our worship services. This is how the New Testament churches worshipped the Lord.

Once the believers in the church in Antioch gathered for worship. As they praised the Lord and fasted, the Holy Spirit spoke and said, "Set apart for me Barnabas and Saul for the work to which I have called them" (Acts 13:2). The Holy Spirt was indeed in charge of their worship service. He set the tone and gave directions on how they were to proceed. The same divine order should mark our worship services today. If we are to truly worship God in Spirit and truth, we must ever allow the Spirit of God to empower and direct our worship.

To do this, it is essential that the human worship leaders be full of the Spirit and able to discern the Spirit's voice. They must remain in constant submission to the Spirit's leading, and they must be careful never to wrest the service out of His hands. It is also necessary that the congregation be taught how to follow and respond to the promptings of the Spirit. If we will do these things, the Spirit will come and direct our worship services "just as he determines" (1 Cor. 12:11). It is only then that we will truly worship God in Spirit and in truth.

Walking with the Holy Spirit

Now that you have concluded today's reading, take a few moments to complete the following exercise.

A Truth to Embrace: I must worship God according to the pattern He has established, that is, in Spirit and in truth.

A Commitment to Make: Since God is Spirit and truth, I commit myself to learn to worship Him in Spirit and in truth.

A Prayer to Pray: Oh Spirit of Truth, fill me now and direct and empower my worship of God.

A Verse to Memorize: "A time is coming and has now come when the true worshipers will worship the Father in spirit and truth, for they are the kind of worshipers the Father seeks. (John 4:23-24)

The Spirit Helps Us Understand the Bible

The night before He was crucified Jesus met with His disciples in an upper room and taught them many things. One thing He taught them was about the coming of the Holy Spirit. He told them that, when He returned to heaven, He would speak to His Father, and the Father would send the Holy Spirit to take His place (John 14:16). Jesus added, "The Holy Spirit, whom the Father will send in my name, will teach you all things and will remind you of everything I have said to you" (v. 26). Later in His message, Jesus explained further, "When he, the Spirit of truth, comes, he will guide you into all truth" (16:13).

Today, we will discover how the Holy Spirit guides us into truth by helping us to understand the Bible.

The Spirit Inspired the Bible

Before we can intelligently discuss how the Holy Spirit helps us understand the Bible, we must first know how He inspired it. Peter wrote, "Above all, you must understand that no prophecy of Scripture [meaning the Bible,] came about by the prophet's own interpretation. For prophecy never had its origin in the will of man, but men spoke from God as they were carried along by the Holy Spirit" (2 Pet. 1:20). Peter is saying that the Holy Spirit moved on the prophets and apostles of old, inspiring them to write the words of Scripture. Paul put it like this: "All Scripture is God-breathed and is useful for teaching, rebuking, correcting, and training in righteousness" (2 Tim. 3:16). Thus, the Holy Spirit is the true Author of Scripture. He is the One who inspired the biblical writers to say what they said.

The Spirit Interprets the Bible

Since the Spirit of God is the Author of the Bible, we can confidently look to Him to help us understand what the Bible teaches. Paul explained this truth to the Christians in Corinth. "We have not received the spirit of the world," he wrote, "but the Spirit who is from God, that we may understand what God has freely given us" (1 Cor. 2:12). The apostle continued, "The man without the Spirit does not accept the things that come from the Spirit of God, for they are foolishness to him, and he cannot understand them, because they are spiritually discerned" (v. 14). In other words, by using our natural minds alone, we can never fully grasp what the Bible teaches. The spiritual truths found in Scripture must be spiritually discerned.

This spiritual discernment comes from the Holy Spirit. John wrote, "The anointing you received from him remains in you, and you do not need anyone to teach you. But...his anointing teaches you about all things" (1 John 2:27). In other words, the Holy Spirit whom we have received will help us understand the Bible.

We must not think, however, that John is saying that our being filled with the Spirit will automatically cause us understand Scripture. Nor must we think he is saying that we should disregard godly, Spirit-anointed teachers. After all, teachers are one of Christ's gifts to the church (1 Cor. 12:28; Eph. 4:11). What John is saying is that we do not have to be dependent on some "priestly class" to understand the Bible. This is because the Holy Spirit dwells in us, and we can depend on Him to help us understand the clear meaning of Scripture. We must, however, still pray and apply ourselves to diligent study the Bible, and we must use sound methods of interpretation. Yet in all of this, we must realize that we are not alone in this endeavor, for the Holy Spirit is with us, and in us, to help guide us into all truth.

The Spirit Helps Us Understand the Bible

How then does the Spirit help us understand the Bible? He helps us in several ways. Let's look briefly at three of those ways.

1. By opening our hearts. First, the Spirit helps us to understand the Bible by opening our hearts to God and causing us to highly esteem His revealed Word. Paul wrote, "The things that come from the Spirit of God [which includes the truths found in Scripture] are foolishness to the person without God's Spirit" (1 Cor. 2:14). However, when a man or woman is born again and filled with the Holy Spirit, the Spirit causes them to love God and to value His message to us in the Bible. As we become better acquainted with the Author of the Bible, we grow to love the Bible more. Like the Psalmist they will cry out to God, "Oh, how I love your law! I meditate on it all day long" (Psa. 119:97).

Once a young woman was given a book of romantic poems. After reading one or two of the poems, she became bored and laid the book aside. Sometime later, she met a young man and fell deeply in love with him, only to discover that he was the poet who wrote the book she had laid aside. She again took up the book and began to read it. However, this time her heart was thrilled as each poem spoke directly to her heart. The book of poems became her most cherished possession. She had fallen in love with the author, and now she loved the book he had written.

It is the same with the Bible. As we grow to love its Author, the more, we grow to cherish the Book He wrote. The Author of the Bible, the Holy Spirit, will make its stories more vivid and its truths more precious.

2. By giving us insight. A second way the Holy Spirit helps us to understand the Bible is by giving us insight into its meaning. Jesus told Nicodemus, "No one can see the kingdom of God unless he is born again" (John 3:3). We are born again when we repent of our sins and trust in Jesus alone for salvation. At that moment, the Spirit of God comes into our being, renews our minds, and begins transforming us into Christ's image (Rom. 12:2; 2 Cor. 3:17-18). Only then are we capable of "correctly handling the word of truth" (2 Tim. 2:15). Jesus said, "When he, the Spirit of truth, comes, he will guide [us] into all truth" (John 16:13). As we prayerfully study the Bible, we can expect the Holy Spirit to come and give us insight into its meaning.

3. By transforming us. Finally, the Holy Spirit will help us to understand the Bible by transforming us and helping us to us obey its teachings. One cannot truly understand the Bible until he or she has, by faith, accepted its teaching and applied them to their own lives. Paul taught that without the Spirit we are powerless to do this. Unless we, with the Spirit's help, do what the Bible teaches, we can never fully understand its teaching.

Paul told the Romans that God's requirement that we live by His Word can be fulfilled in us, "who do not live according to the sinful nature but according to the Spirit" (Rom. 8:4). As we, through the Spirit's power, do what the Word of God says, we come to better understand what it means. Oh, how we need the Spirit of God to fill us and help us understand and apply the teachings of the Bible to our lives.

Walking with the Holy Spirit

A Truth to Embrace: I cannot fully understand and apply the teachings of Scripture without the help of the Spirit.

A Commitment to Make: I commit myself to prayerfully open my heart to the Spirit of Truth as I study Scripture.

A Prayer to Pray: Dear Holy Spirit, come and fill me now. Help me to better understand God's word and to apply it to my life.

A Verse to Memorize: "When he, the Spirit of truth, comes, he will guide you into all truth." (John 16:13)

The Spirit Helps Us Become Like Jesus

One day, Jesus was walking through His hometown of Nazareth. He passed a man named Matthew sitting at his table collecting taxes. Jesus looked at Matthew and said to him, "Follow me." Immediately, Matthew got up and followed Jesus. (Matt. 9:9). This is but one of twenty times in the four gospels that Jesus issued the command to "Follow me."

Christianity is more than a decision to receive Jesus as Savoir. It involves our leaving all to follow Him. We are to go after Him with all our hearts, patterning our lives on His beautiful life. To become more like Him must become our life's ambition.

On Day 14, we looked at how the Spirit helps us to represent Christ to a lost world by filling us with God's love, and by creating in us the character of Christ. Today, we will look a little deeper into how the Holy Spirit helps us to become like Jesus.

Called to Live Like Jesus

John wrote, "Whoever claims to live in him must walk as Jesus did" (1 John 2:6). Peter reminds us that Christ left us an example, and we should "follow in his steps" (1 Pet. 2:21). Paul told the Philippian believers, "Your attitude should be the same as that of Christ Jesus" (Phil. 2:5). These apostles are telling us that, as Christians, our chief purpose in life is to become like Christ. This raises the question, "If we are called to live like Jesus, then what kind of life did He live?

1. Jesus lived a life of purity. Peter, who walked with Jesus for three years, wrote, "He committed no sin, and no deceit was found in his mouth" (1 Pet. 2:22). John, who also walked closely with Jesus, testified, "In him is no sin" (1 John 3:5).

2. Jesus also lived a life of selflessness. He spent His life caring for others. Paul said that for our sakes Jesus "made himself nothing, taking the very nature of a servant" (Phil. 2:7). He now commands us, "As I have loved you, so you must love one another" (John 13:34). Our Lord went even further, saying, "You have heard that it was said, 'Love your neighbor and hate your enemy.' But I tell you: Love your enemies and pray for those who persecute you, that you may be sons of your Father in heaven" (Matt. 5:43-45).

3. Jesus lived a life of commitment to His Father's will. "My food," He testified, "is to do the will of him who sent me and to finish his work" (John 4:34). This commitment ultimately took Jesus to the cross. In the Garden of Gethsemane, He pondered the agony He would suffer on the cross. Yet, He prayed to His Heavenly Father, "Not my will, but yours be done" (Luke 22:42).

The Bible calls us to imitate Christ in His purity, His selflessness, and His commitment to His Father's mission. Peter wrote, "Just as he who called you is holy, so be holy in all you do" (1 Pet. 1:15-16).

An Impossible Assignment

When we hear this, we are tempted to wring our hands in despair. How can we as mere humans ever live like Jesus? It is a seemingly impossible assignment. The apostle Paul must have had similar feelings when he wrote, "I have the desire to do what is good, but I cannot carry it out" (Rom. 7:18). To live like Jesus was a task beyond his ability—and ours. How then can we ever hope to live such exemplary lives? How can we even hope to master our inclination to sin and self-centeredness? Can we ever find the moral and spiritual courage we need to commit our lives fully to God and His mission? Yes, we can! We can do it the same way Jesus did it—in the power of the Holy Spirit.

The Bible says that, when Jesus was baptized, "the Holy Spirit descended on him in bodily form like a dove" (Luke 3:22). Soon afterward, the Spirit led Him into the Judean wilderness where, through the Spirit's power, He overcame the devil's temptations. Jesus then revealed the source of His strength by announcing, "The Spirit of the Lord is on me, because he has anointed me…" (Luke 4:18). Peter added, "God anointed Jesus of Nazareth with the Holy Spirit and power, and…he went around doing good" (Acts 10:38). The Holy Spirit thus empowered Jesus to do His Father's will and fulfill His God-given mission.

Paul also described how the Spirit helped him. When faced with his own inability to live a holy life, he cried out in despair, "What a wretched man I am! Who will rescue me from this body of death?" (Rom. 7:24). He then answered His own question: "Thanks be to God, through Jesus Christ our Lord!" (v. 25). Paul went on to explain that one could have power over sin by living "according to the Spirit" (Rom. 8:5).

How the Holy Spirit Helps Us

This insight presents us with another important question, "How does the Holy Spirit help us to live as Christ lived?" The Spirit helps us in at least two ways:

1. New creations. First, when we receive Jesus as our Savior, the Spirit comes, regenerates us, and makes us into new creations in Christ. Paul wrote that before we were saved, our lives were "controlled by the sinful nature" (Rom. 7:5). Because of this, our hearts were naturally drawn toward sinful deeds and thoughts. However, when we were born again, the Spirit of Christ entered our beings and began to produce in us the character of Jesus. We now want to live pure, selfless, and committed lives. This life is characterized by love, joy, peace, patience, kindness, goodness, faithfulness, gentleness, and self-control. Paul called these character traits the "fruit of the Spirit" (Gal. 5:33). We will look more closely at these fruit of the Spirit on Day 30.

2. Power for life. A second way the Holy Spirit enables us to live like Jesus is by giving us the power we need to live for Him. Paul told the Corinthian believers that they were to live "in purity…in the Holy Spirit… and in the power of God" (2 Cor. 6:6). When we are saved, the Spirit comes and indwells us. Then, when we are baptized in the Holy Spirit, He comes to empower us as Christ's witnesses. That witness includes both our words and our deeds. Now, if we will submit ourselves to the Spirit, He will enable us to speak and live in such a way that people "may see [our] good deeds and praise [our] Father in heaven" (Matt. 5:16).

Paul reminded the Roman Christians, "You…are controlled not by the sinful nature but by the Spirit" (Rom. 8:9). In another place, he exhorted believers, "Live by the Spirit, and you will not gratify the desires of the sinful nature." (Gal. 5:16). To live by the Spirit, one must be born of the Spirit, filled with the Spirit, and live daily under the Spirit's power and guidance.

Walking with the Holy Spirit

Now that you have concluded today's reading, take a few moments to complete the following exercise.

A Truth to Embrace: The Holy Spirit will empower me, enabling me to live more like Jesus.

A Commitment to Make: I will allow the Holy Spirit to work in my life molding me into the image of Christ.

A Prayer to Pray: Dear Holy Spirit, take all of me, spirit, soul, and body. Show me how I must change to become more like Jesus. Then, empower me to make those changes.

A Verse to Memorize: "Those who live according to the sinful nature have their minds set on what that nature desires; but those who live in accordance with the Spirit have their minds set on what the Spirit desires." (Rom. 8:5)

Day 25

The Spirit Encourages and Guides Us

T he night before He was crucified, Jesus gathered His disciples in an upper room in Jerusalem. He told them that He would soon leave them. He then promised to send Someone to take His place. "I will ask the Father," He said, "and he will give you another Helper, to be with you forever" (John 14:16-17, ESV). He added, "I will not leave you as orphans; I will come to you" (v. 18). About six weeks later, soon before He returned to heaven, Jesus made another promise to His disciples: "Surely I am with you always, to the very end of the age" (Matt. 28:20).

On both occasions, Jesus was talking about the Holy Spirit, whom He would send on the Day of Pentecost (Acts 2:1-4; 33). Today, we will discover how the Holy Spirit, as Jesus' representative, will fulfill Jesus' promise to come along side us to cheer, encourage, and direct us.

The Spirit Will Encourage Us

In the gospel of John, when Jesus referred to the Holy Spirit as "another Helper," He used the Greek phrase, *allos Parakletos.* In using these words, Jesus was saying that He would send another One, just like Him, who would walk alongside His followers to encourage and empower them to serve Him more perfectly. He was telling them that the Holy Spirit would come to them as their ever-present Helper, Encourager, and Guide. What a great comfort this must have been to Christ's first followers.

And how wonderful it is today to know that the Holy Spirit is walking beside us and dwelling in us. This reality brings great encouragement into our hearts, especially when we encounter opposition to the cause of Christ. Whatever the situation, we can know that the Holy Spirit will enable us to confidently face any difficulty, endure any trail, and emerge victoriously in Christ. This is yet another reason for us to be filled with, and remain full of, the Holy Spirit.

The Spirit Will Speak to Us

Not only will the Holy Spirit come to us to encourage us, on occasion, He will speak to us and tell us what we should do and say. Jesus told His disciples, "When you are brought before synagogues, rulers and authorities, do not worry about how you will defend yourselves or what you will say, for the Holy Spirit will teach you at that time what you should say" (Luke 12:11-12).

Once, Paul was ministering in the city of Corinth. Because of the difficulty of the work, he became discouraged. Then one night the Spirit gave Paul a vision. In the vision, the Lord Jesus appeared and spoke to Paul, saying. "Do not be afraid; keep on speaking, do not be silent. For I am with you, and no one is going to attack and harm you, because I have many people in this city" (Acts 18:9-10). Paul was encouraged and remained in Corinth for another year and a half preaching the gospel. Thus, a great church was established in the city. The same can be true for us today. If we will remain full of the Holy Spirit and live prayerful committed lives, the Spirit of God will speak to us too.

How to Hear the Spirit's Voice

An important question we must answer is, "How can one hear and know the Spirit's voice when He does speak?" To be able to hear the Spirit's voice, we must first understand the ways He speaks to us. Primarily, the Holy Spirit speaks to us through the book He inspired, the Holy Bible. As we prayerfully read and reflect on the words of Scripture, the Spirit of Truth will open our hearts and use those words to show us what we should do.

On occasions, the Spirit may also speak to us through dreams, visions, and prophetic words as He did in the New Testament. Most usually, however, God speaks to our spirits by His Spirit. Isaiah described it like this: "Your ears will hear a voice behind you saying, 'This is the way; walk in it'" (Isa. 30:20). Paul affirmed, "Those who are led by the Spirit of God are the sons of God" and that "the Spirit himself testifies with our spirit that we are God's children" (Rom. 8:14, 16).

As God's children, we can expect the Spirit to guide us in these ways. We must never forget, however, that God's Spirit will never tell us to do anything that contradicts what He has already said in the Bible.

To hear the Spirit's voice, we must prepare our hearts. Scripture counsels, "Today, if you will hear his voice, do not harden your hearts" (Heb. 3:7-8). We ought to always keep our hearts open and tender before God. Such sensitivity to the Spirit rises from a humble and obedient heart. And it comes through a consistent devotional life, including time spent in prayer and meditation on the Word.

Finally, if we are to learn to recognize the voice of the Spirit, we must by faith practice obeying His voice when He speaks. We really have but one good reason to hear the Spirit's voice. We hear His voice in order that we might obey it. As we obey and follow His instructions, we learn to better discern His voice.

Walking with the Holy Spirit

Now that you have concluded today's reading, take a few moments to complete the following exercise.

A Truth to Embrace: If I will live a prayerful, obedient life, the Holy Spirit will walk with me to encourage and guide me along the way.

A Commitment to Make: I commit myself to learn how to better discern the voice of the Spirit when He speaks to me.

A Prayer to Pray: Dear Holy Spirit, fill me now, and help me to understand who You are and what You want to do in my life.

A Verse to Memorize: "For those who are led by the Spirit of God are the children of God." (Rom. 8:14)

Part 7

Living and Ministering
in the Spirit

Day 26

Speaking in Tongues: Its Blessing and Benefits

A young man was hungry for more of God. He wanted to be empowered by the Spirit so he could more effectively serve the Lord. However, when he was told that he should expect to speak in tongues when was baptized in the Holy Spirit, he became troubled.

"Do I *have* to speak in tongues?" he asked, "What good is speaking tongues anyway?" Today, we will answer this young man's question. We will discuss some of the blessings and benefits that come into a Christian's life through prayer in tongues.

What Is Speaking in Tongues?

While most Christians know that speaking in tongues is found in the Bible, few have a clear understanding of its nature and purpose. On Day 18, we learned that speaking in tongues is the "initial physical evidence" of one's being baptized in the Holy Spirit. However, speaking in tongues is much more than a mere evidence that one has been filled with the Holy Spirit.

In fact, speaking in tongues was a common practice of early Christians. The New Testament speaks of the practice in five different passages. In His Great Commission, Jesus told His disciples that believers would speak in tongues (Mark 16:17). Later, when the Holy Spirit was poured out on the Day of Pentecost, the Bible says that all of the disciples "were filled with the Holy Spirit and began to speak in other tongues as the Spirit enabled them" (Acts 2:4). Two more times the Book of Acts tells of believers speaking in tongues upon receiving the Holy Spirit (10:46; 19:6). In 1 Corinthians, Paul taught in detail about the gift of tongues (12:10, 28, 30; 13:1, 8; 14:5-6, 18, 21-23, 39). And finally, in Romans 8, Paul was likely referring to tongues when he said, "The Spirit himself intercedes for us with groans that words cannot express" (v. 26; cf. 1 Cor. 14:14). The Bible further teaches that speaking in tongues will continue as a practice in the church until Jesus comes again to establish His perfect kingdom in the earth (Acts 2:39; 1 Cor. 13:8-10).

The young man asked, "What good is speaking in tongues?" Speaking in tongues is a wonderful spiritual experience that occurs when the Spirit of God moves freely on the spirit of a yielded believer (1 Cor. 14:14). Under the Spirit's impulse the Spirit-filled believer speaks in a language he or she does not know (Acts 2:1-4). Paul described speaking in tongues as a "manifestation of the Spirit" (1 Cor. 12:7). It is thus a supernatural experience coming from the Spirit of God. The words spoken can be in any human language or dialect (Acts 2:8), or they can be a heavenly language (1 Cor. 13:1). The Bible teaches that every believer should desire to speak in tongues (Mark 16:17; Acts 2:4; 1 Cor. 14:5).

Speaking in tongues can bring great blessing to both the church in general and individual believers in particular. It can do this in three important ways: It can serve as a sign to believers and nonbelievers; it can assist Christians in their private devotions; and it can serve as a means of strengthening the church. Let's look at each of these benefits of speaking in tongues.

Tongues Are a Sign

When someone is baptized in the Holy Spirit, he or she will speak in tongues as the Spirit gives utterance (Acts 2:4). This miraculous, Spirit-inspired speech in an unlearned language serves as a sign to that person, and to the entire congregation of believers, that he or she has been empowered to speak for Christ. It is the first fulfillment of Jesus' promise in Acts 1:8: "You will receive power when the Holy Spirit comes on you; and you will be my witnesses." (We will discuss this more tomorrow.)

Speaking in tongues also serves as a "sign to unbelievers" who witness the event (1 Cor. 14:22). When unbelievers hear a follower of Christ speaking in tongues, they are made aware that God is present and that His Spirit is moving among God's people. In ancient times, a clarion call signaled that a herald was about to make an important announcement. In much the same way, an utterance in tongues can serve as a signal to the unlearned that something important and supernatural is taking place.

This is what happened on the Day of Pentecost. When the crowds heard the disciples speaking in tongues, they were "bewildered" and "amazed" (vv.6-7). Their hearts were opened and made ready to hear Peter proclaim the gospel.

Tongues in Private Devotions

Prayer in tongues is also of great benefit to one's personal spiritual life. During times of private devotion, Spirit-inspired tongues can function as a personal prayer language. As one prays in tongues, he or she is made acutely aware of the Spirit's dynamic presence within. Such an awareness can become a source of great confidence and joy.

Paul said, "He who speaks in a tongue edifies himself" (1 Cor. 14:4). Jude exhorted believers to "build yourselves up in your most holy faith, and pray in the Holy Spirit" (v. 20). To pray in tongues, a believer must put his or her confidence in God, and they must yield themselves completely to the Holy Spirit. As they do these things, they learn to more fully trust in God and His grace.

Tongues are further a perfect outlet for praise and worship. Paul taught that the person who speaks in an unknown tongue is "praising God with [his or her] spirit" and giving thanks to Him (1 Cor. 14:16).

Finally, as we discussed on Day 21, prayer in tongues can sometimes function as a means of intercessory prayer. Paul talked about this kind of prayer in Romans 8. He said that, as humans, we are limited in our ability to pray as we should. The Spirit, however, offers to help us. Paul writes, "But the Spirit himself intercedes for us with groans that words cannot express" (v. 26). The Spirit thus intercedes through us in words of His choosing, and He does so "in accordance with God's will" (v. 27).

Tongues in Public Worship

Tongues can also properly function as a gift of the Holy Spirit in public worship (1 Cor. 12:10, 28). In 1 Corinthians 12-14, Paul instructed the church concerning the proper use of the gift. In this context, the gift of tongues is to be exercised in combination with the gift of the interpretation of tongues (1 Cor. 14:5, 27). These two spiritual gifts thus work together to build up the church (vv. 12, 26).

When properly exercised, they bless the congregation in two significant ways. On some occasions, the Spirit may use these gifts to communicate divine truth and insight to God's people. On other occasions, He may inspire individuals to offer up Spirit-directed prayers on behalf of the congregation. In either case, the result is that the church is strengthened.

Prayer in tongues, whether used in private devotions or in public worship, can be a great spiritual blessing. We should not neglect the use of this wonderful gift from God.

Walking with the Holy Spirit

Now that you have concluded today's reading, take a few moments to complete the following exercise.

A Truth to Embrace: Speaking in tongues is a wonderful gift from God's Spirit through which He confirms His work in individuals, strengthens Christians, and along with the gift of the interpretation of tongues, builds up the church.

A Commitment to Make: I will allow the Holy Spirit to pray through me during my times of personal devotion and intercessory prayer. And I will be open to His using me in the manifestation of the gifts of tongues and the interpretation of tongues in public worship.

A Prayer to Pray: Dear Holy Spirit, fill me now, and super-naturally pray through me with the words You give.

A Verse to Memorize: "What is it then? I will pray with the spirit, and I will pray with the understanding also: I will sing with the spirit, and I will sing with the understanding also." (1 Cor. 14:15, KJV)

Day 27

Ministry in the Spirit

Someone has rightly observed that we can do the work of God in one of two ways. We can do it in our own strength, or we can do it in the Spirit's strength. Jesus and the early Christians chose to minister in the Spirit's strength. As a result, they ministered with great power and authority. In this lesson, we will learn how we too can appropriate the Spirit's power in our own ministries today.

The Spirit Empowers

We must begin by knowing how the Holy Spirit empowers us for ministry. At the end of His ministry on earth, Jesus issued two parting commands. First, He ordered His followers to preach the gospel to all nations (Mark 16:16-18). This command is known as the "Great Commission." Jesus then ordered them to wait in Jerusalem until they had been empowered by the Holy Spirit (Acts 1:4-8). This mandate has been called Christ's "Final Command." Jesus knew that, before they could fulfill His Great Commission command, they would need to obey His Final Command.

The same is true for us today. We too must be empowered by the Holy Spirit to effectively carry out Jesus' commission. The ministries of Jesus and the early believers serve as models of how we should minister today.

The ministry of Jesus. Jesus came to earth to offer himself up as a ransom for all people (Matt. 20:28). He also came to show us how we should live and minister in the Spirit's power (John 13:15, 14:12, 16). Jesus began His ministry by being anointed by the Holy Spirit (Luke 4:18-19). He then went out and ministered in the Spirit's power (Acts 10:38). In doing this, He set the pattern for all who would follow in His footsteps (John 14:12).

The ministry of the early believers. Like Jesus, the early church ministered in the power of the Holy Spirit. They were first empowered on the Day of Pentecost (Acts 2:4). They then went out and ministered with great power and effectiveness. They were simply following the pattern set by Jesus—first be empowered, then minister. We, too, have been called to minister in the power of the Holy Spirit, just as did Jesus and the early believers.

The Spirit Enables

Not only does the Holy Spirit empower us for ministry, He enables us in ministry. He does this in at least four ways:

1. Inspiring. First, the Spirit inspires us to do ministry. In the Book of Act, the Holy Spirit inspired Peter to go to Caesarea and preach to the Gentiles there. When the Jewish Christians asked him why he did this, Peter answered, "The Holy Spirit told me to go with them and not to worry that they were Gentiles" (Acts 11:12, NLT). He will do the same for us today. He will give a burden for the lost, a love for the church, and a vision for the world.

2. Empowering. Next, the Spirit empowers our witness to the lost. Jesus promised, "You will receive power when the Holy Spirit comes on you; and you will be my witnesses" (Acts 1:8). We can become powerful witnesses for Christ only if we will allow the Holy Spirit to fill us and use us in His harvest field. This empowering includes an ability to speak persuasively (Acts 6:10) and gifts of the Holy Spirit to supernaturally confirm the word (Acts 8:6).

3. Anointing. Third, the Spirit anoints our preaching and teaching. We will discuss this aspect of the Spirit's enablement tomorrow.

4. Gifting. Finally, the Spirit will manifest himself through spiritual gifts. The outpouring of the Spirit at Pentecost resulted in a dramatic release of miraculous power in the disciples' ministries. This release of power manifested itself in speaking in tongues, prophetic preaching, powerful healings, signs and wonders, exorcisms, supernatural deliverances, dreams, visions, and Holy Spirit baptisms. Today, if we will be filled with the Spirit, and boldly proclaim Christ to the lost, we too can expect the same supernatural confirmations.

Appropriating the Spirit's Help

How then can we appropriate the Spirit's help in ministry? We can do this in three ways. First, we can secure the Spirit's help *by being filled with the Spirit.* The empowering of the Holy Spirit is an essential requirement for all spiritual ministry (Acts 1:4-5, 8). We can further ensure the Spirit's help in ministry *by walking in step with in the Spirit* (Gal. 5:25). We do this by living lives of prayer, holiness, and yieldedness to the Spirit of God.

Finally, we can secure the Spirit's aid in ministry *by appropriate-ing the Spirit's help.* As we walk in the Spirit, we can expect ministry opportunities to come our way. At such times, we can depend on the Holy Spirit to direct on how we should respond. When He does, we must act in obedience and faith. These two elements—obedience and faith—are key to releasing the Spirit's power in ministry. When we act in obedience to the Word of God and the inner promptings of the

Spirit, He comes and anoints us for ministry. For example, as we obey Christ's command to witness, the Spirit comes upon us and empowers us.

However, the opposite is also true. If we disobey, and refuse to witness, the anointing does not come. Many Christians have failed to become effective witnesses for Christ simply because they have refused to obey His command to witness to those with whom they come into contact. The principle is this: we must first obey, *then* the Spirit comes to enable us. This principle applies not only to witnessing but to any ministry situation.

Here's how it works: The Spirit-filled disciple discerns the Spirit's voice prompting him or her to minister. They now have a choice; they can obey the Spirit's voice, or they can ignore it. If they obey, the anointing comes. If, however, they disobey, the anointing subsides. Once the Christian worker commits to obey the Spirit's voice and begins to minister, he or she must then act in faith. Through a bold act of faith, the anointing is released, the work is accomplished, and the need is met.

Walking with the Holy Spirit

Now that you have concluded today's reading, take a few moments to complete the following exercise.

A Truth to Embrace: Because the same Spirit who anointed Jesus and the apostles also anoints me, I can minister in the Spirit's power just as they did.

A Commitment to Make: I commit myself to walk in the Spirit and listen for His voice. When He speaks, I will obey and trust Him to do the work.

A Prayer to Pray: Dear Holy Spirit, fill me again, and anoint me to minister in Your power.

A Verse to Memorize: "And these signs will accompany those who believe: In my name they will drive out demons; they will speak in new tongues; they will pick up snakes with their hands; and when they drink deadly poison, it will not hurt them at all; they will place their hands on sick people, and they will get well." (Mark 16:17-18)

Day 28

Spirit-Anointed Preaching and Teaching

Have you ever been deeply moved by the words of a preacher or teacher? Did you stop and ask yourself why you were so moved? A number of factors can cause a minister's message to be effective. One important element is the touch of God, or to put it another way, the anointing of the Holy Spirit. Today, we will consider the importance of a minister being anointed by the Holy Spirit. We will further examine how one may assure that he or she is anointed when they minister the Word of God.

Jesus Set the Pattern

Jesus set the pattern for how we should minister God's word. Our teaching and preaching should be done in the Spirit's power. Jesus described His own teaching ministry like this: "I do nothing on my own, but speak just what the Father has taught me" (John 8:28). Jesus could clearly hear His Father's voice because He was full of the Holy Spirit. He began His ministry by announcing, "The Spirit of the Lord is on me, because he has anointed me to preach good news to the poor. He has sent me to proclaim freedom for the prisoners and recovery of sight for the blind, to release the oppressed, to proclaim the year of the Lord's favor" (Luke 4:18-19). On another occasion Jesus declared, "The words I have spoken to you are spirit and they are life" (John 6:63). Because Jesus was anointed by the Holy Spirit, the words He spoke were powerful and grace-filled.

Once Jesus had announced that the Spirit of the Lord was upon Him, He began to proclaim the good news. The Bible says that, "All spoke well of him and were amazed at the gracious words that came from his lips" (Luke 4:22). One day the Jewish authorities sent some temple guards to capture Jesus and bring Him to them. However, when the guards returned, Jesus was not with them. The authorities asked, "Why didn't you bring Jesus to us as we ordered?" The guards replied, "No one ever spoke the way this man does!" (John 7:46). They had been awed by Jesus' Spirit-anointed words.

The Apostles Followed the Pattern

The apostles followed the pattern established by Jesus. They too ministered in the power of the Holy Spirit. The Bible says that, on the Day of Pentecost, "all of them were filled with the Holy Spirit and began to speak in other tongues as the Spirit enabled them" (Acts 2:4). Because of this powerful spiritual experience, they were anointed by the Holy Spirit, just as Jesus had been when the Spirit came upon Him at His baptism (Luke 3:21-22). And like Jesus, they began to teach and preach with power. After receiving the Spirit at Pentecost, Peter stood and proclaimed the gospel. His Spirit-laden words made such an impression on his listeners that they were "cut to the heart" and began to cry out, "What shall we do?" (Acts 2:37).

Throughout the Book of Acts, the other apostles and preachers spoke with the same power and effect. When the Holy Spirit was poured out a second time in Jerusalem, they were again "all filled with the Holy Spirit and spoke the word of God boldly" (Acts 4:31). The apostles then "with great power...continued to testify to the resurrection of the Lord Jesus, and much grace was upon them all" (v. 33). Later in Acts, when Paul was filled with the Holy Spirit, "at once he began to preach in the synagogues that Jesus is the Son of God" (Acts 9:20). His powerful, Spirit-anointed preaching "baffled the Jews living in Damascus...proving that Jesus is the Christ" (v. 22).

Years later, in a letter to the believers in Corinth, Paul reminded them how he had preached the gospel to them. "My message and my preaching were not with wise and persuasive words," he wrote, "but with a demonstration of the Spirit's power" (1 Cor. 2:4).

Following the Pattern Today

Today, we should follow the pattern established by Jesus and His apostles. We too should teach and preach in the power of the Spirit. Paul wrote that God "has made us competent as ministers of a new covenant—not of the letter but of the Spirit; for the letter kills, but the Spirit gives life" (2 Cor. 3:6). What then must we do that we may become competent, Spirit-anointed teachers and preachers of the word of the Lord? We must do at least five things:

1. Be born of the Spirit. First, we must be born from above. Before one can minister in the Spirit's power, he or she must be born of the Spirit. Jesus explained, "Flesh gives birth to flesh, but the Spirit gives birth to spirit" (John 3:7).

2. Be filled with the Spirit. Next, before we can preach or teach with power, we must be filled with the Spirit. This is what happened to Jesus and the apostles. It was only after the Spirit came upon them and anointed them that they began to minister in power. Jesus commanded His disciples to be His witnesses to all nations. But first,

He said, they were to remain in the city of Jerusalem until they had been "clothed with power from on high" (Luke 24:48-49). The disciples obeyed, and on the Day of Pentecost they received the promised power. We must do the same.

3. Walk in the Spirit. Third, preparation for Spirit-empowered proclamation involves daily walking in the Spirit's power. It is one thing to be initially filled with the Spirit, it is quite another to walk in the Spirit. We do this by being daily refilled with the Spirit. This Spirit-empowered walk is nourished through committed prayer and disciplined Christian living.

4. Focus on the gospel. Fourth, if we are to preach and teach with power, we must *stay focused on the gospel,* that is, the message of salvation in Christ. Paul called this message "the power of God for the salvation of everyone who believes" (Rom. 1:16). Remember, the Spirit does not anoint our message but God's, that is, the good news that Jesus died on the cross for the sins of all people.

5. Depend on the Spirit. Finally, if we are to minister with power, we must learn to depend on the Spirit. In other words, we must teach and preach with faith and expectancy. As we speak, we should believe that God will fulfill His promise and anoint our words just as He anointed the words of Jesus, Peter, and Paul. We should further expect the Spirit to work in the hearts of those listening to our words, and that their lives will be transformed by the Spirit of God and by the message of the gospel.

Walking with the Holy Spirit

Now that you have concluded today's reading, take a few moments to complete the following exercise.

A Truth to Embrace: When I teach, preach, or otherwise share God's word, I should seek to be anointed by the Holy Spirit.

Day 28: Spirit-Anointed Preaching and Teaching

A Commitment to Make: I commit myself to seek Your empowering each time I share Your word.

A Prayer to Pray: Holy Spirit, come upon me, and fill me that I may teach and preach Your word more effectively.

A Verse to Memorize: "The Spirit of the Lord is on me, because he has anointed me to proclaim good news to the poor. He has sent me to proclaim freedom for the prisoners and recovery of sight for the blind, to set the oppressed free, to proclaim the year of the Lord's favor." (Luke 4:18-19)

Day 29

Gifts of the Spirit

During His days on earth, people were attracted to Jesus by His gracious words (John 6:63), His mighty works (Mark 2:45; Luke 4:25), and His beautiful life (Mark 7:37). Today, as God's missionary people, we are called to represent Christ to lost humanity. We seek to attract people to Him and His church. We can do this by exhibiting in our lives the same three qualities Jesus exhibited in His: gracious words, mighty works, and beautiful lives.

The Spirit will enable us to do this by giving to us spiritual gifts and spiritual fruit. Through these gifts and fruit, the Spirit enables us to display the full character of Christ. Through the exercise of spiritual gifts, we are enabled to declare the powerful words and display the mighty works of Jesus. Through the manifestation of spiritual fruit, we are enabled to emulate His beautiful life. Today, we will focus on the gifts of the Holy Spirit. Tomorrow, we will focus on the fruit.

Defining Spiritual Gifts

In 1 Corinthians 12:8-10, Paul lists nine gifts (or "manifestations") of the Spirit. He says,

Now to each one the manifestation of the Spirit is given for the common good. To one there is given through the Spirit the message of wisdom, to another the message of knowledge by means of the same Spirit, to another faith by the same Spirit, to another gifts of healing by that one Spirit, to another miraculous powers, to another prophecy, to another distinguishing between spirits, to another speaking in different kinds of tongues, and to still another the interpretation of tongues. (1 Cor. 12:7-10)

These gifts represent the various ways the Spirit of God manifests His presence and power in the midst of His people. These nine gifts of the Spirit can be defined as *supernatural anointings given by the Spirit of God through Spirit-filled believers to accomplish the will of the Father.* In his epistles, Paul introduces and names the gifts. In the Book of Acts, Luke demonstrates them in action. By comparing what each biblical author teaches about these gifts, we get a full picture of what they are and how they are manifested. We further discover that God gives these gifts for two purposes, to build up the church and to advance His kingdom in the earth.

Categorizing Spiritual Gifts

Bible scholars often place these nine spiritual gifts into three categories, with three gifts in each category. The three categories are revelation gifts, power gifts, and prophetic gifts.

1. Revelation gifts. The revelation gifts are word of knowledge, word of wisdom, and distinguishing between spirits. These three gifts are given so that the Spirit might reveal to His people something He wants them to know.

2. Power gifts. The three power gifts are the gift of faith, gifts of healing, and the gift of miraculous powers. These gifts are given so

166

that the Spirit can work through His people to display God's mighty power and to accomplish a work He wants done.

3. Prophetic gifts. The three prophetic gifts are prophecy, different kinds of tongues, and the interpretation of tongues. These vocal gifts are given so that God may speak through His servants a message He wants someone to hear.

Manifesting Spiritual Gifts

Every follower of Jesus should desire spiritual gifts, and we should all anticipate releasing them in ministry (1 Cor. 12:7). But how may we do this?

We can begin by realizing that spiritual gifts are simply manifestations of the Spirit of God who indwells and empowers the committed follower of Jesus. When a person is born again, the Holy Spirit enters and takes up residence inside that person. Later, when he or she is baptized in the Holy Spirit, the Spirit of God fills them and empowers them to do God's work. As a result of these two potent spiritual experiences, the Holy Spirit is powerfully at work inside them. Moreover, since all the gifts reside in the Spirit, it is reasonable to assume that, if one is full of the Holy Spirit, he or she has all the gifts residing inside them.

Consequently, if we will walk in the Spirit, then the Spirit of God can use us in any way He sees fit. He can release through us any gift He chooses. The question one must therefore ask is not, "What is my spiritual gift?" but "How can I live in such a way that the Spirit can manifest His gifts in my life as they are needed?"

We must further realize that spiritual gifts come as "anointings" from the Holy Spirit. In other words, the Spirit comes upon and works through an individual believer for a brief period to release God's power and grace into a situation.

This is what happened to Paul in the city of Paphos. He was being opposed by a sorcerer named Elymas. In response, the Holy Spirit filled Paul and revealed to him what God was about to do. Paul spoke directly to Elymas and said, "Now the hand of the Lord is against you. You are going to be blind, and for a time you will be unable to see the light of the sun" (Acts 13:11). Then, when the miracle occurred as Paul had predicted, the governor, Sergius Paulus, was amazed and turned to the Lord. In this instance, Paul was likely manifesting the spiritual gift known as a word of knowledge.

Thus, when the Holy Spirit wants to manifest Himself through a particular spiritual gift, He will come as an anointing on a yielded believer. Once the believer senses the anointing, it is his or her duty to act in faith to release the spiritual gift. The act of faith could be to say or do a particular thing. This could be a humanly impossible act. Nevertheless, the believer must step out in faith. Once he or she takes such a step of faith, the anointing is released, the spiritual gift is manifested, and the work is accomplished.

We should all eagerly desire to be used by the Holy Spirit in the manifestation of spiritual gifts (1 Cor. 12:31).

Walking with the Holy Spirit

Now that you have concluded today's reading, take a few moments to complete the following exercise.

A Truth to Embrace: The Holy Spirit wants to manifest spiritual gifts through me.

A Commitment to Make: I commit myself to cultivate a desire for spiritual gifts and to prepare myself to be used in their manifestation.

A Prayer to Pray: Lord, I commit myself to You and to Your kingdom. Fill me with the Spirit and work through me in the manifestation of spiritual gifts.

A Verse to Memorize: "Now to each one the manifestation of the Spirit is given for the common good." (1 Cor. 12:7)

Day 29: Gifts of the Spirit

Day 30

Fruit of the Spirit

It is sometimes debated among believers which is the most needed in the Christian life—the gifts of the Spirit or the fruit of the Spirit. This, however, is a pointless argument. The obvious answer is that both are necessary. True Christian witness involves both manifesting spiritual gifts and exhibiting spiritual fruit. As the gifts and fruit of the Spirit appear together in the Christian's life, his or her witness to the world becomes greater. At the same time, the believer's benefit to the church increases. In the last chapter, we discussed the nine gifts of the Spirit found in 1 Corinthian 12:8-10. In this chapter, we will look at the nine fruit of the Spirit found in Galatians 5:22-23.

Identifying the Fruit of the Spirit

Paul warned the Galatians about yielding to the "desires of the sinful nature." He rather urged them to pursue the "fruit of the Spirit." He writes, "The fruit of the Spirit is love, joy, peace, patience, kindness, goodness, faithfulness, gentleness, and self-control. Against such things there is no law" (Gal. 5:22-23). These fruit of the Spirit can be defined as *Christ-like qualities of character that are produced in believers as they live their lives under the Spirit's influence.* They are Spirit-engendered graces associated with godly attitudes, character, and life-style.

We should not confuse these spiritual fruit with mere human refinements acquired through self-effort. On the contrary, spiritual fruit has its origin in the character of Christ, and they are produced as the Holy Spirit works in one's life. The fruit of the Spirit spring supernaturally from a life yielded to the Spirit of God.

Understanding the Fruit of the Spirit

Like spiritual gifts, spiritual fruit serve to build up the body of Christ and to advance the kingdom of God in the earth. As believers grow in the grace and knowledge of Christ, Christ's character is reproduced in their lives. When people on the outside see these qualities in the Christian community, they are attracted to Christ, the church grows, and God's kingdom advances.

Like spiritual gifts, spiritual fruit are acquired by faith. Unlike spiritual gifts, however, spiritual fruit must be cultivated and grow in the Christian life. They are not manifested in full at the moment of faith, as are spiritual gifts, but grow gradually in the believer's life as a result of his daily submitting to the Spirit and abiding in Christ (Gal. 5:16-25; John 15:1-8).

Fruit of the Spirit in a believer's life indicates that that person is attaining to maturity in Christ. Christian maturity is the quality of having the character and attitudes of Christ. Paul told the Philippian believers, "Your attitude should be the same as that of Christ Jesus" (Phil. 2:5).

The nine fruit of the Spirit perfectly portray the attitudes and character of Christ. When these qualities are present in a believer's life, we can say that that person is a mature Christian. We can further say that he or she is a truly spiritual person. In the words of Paul, the person who is truly spiritual is the one who has "crucified the sinful nature with its

172

passions and desires" (v. 24), is walking "in step with the Spirit" (v. 25), and is displaying the fruit of the Spirit in his or her life (vv. 22-23).

Cultivating the Fruit of the Spirit

How then can a Christian ensure that the fruit of the Spirit are growing in his or her life? We can begin by reminding ourselves that spiritual fruit can only be cultivated by spiritual means. The development of spiritual fruit must therefore begin with spiritual experience. As one is born of the Spirit and filled with the Spirit, the seeds of spiritual fruit are planted in his or her life. For these seeds to grow and produce a harvest, the soil must then be cultivated.

We can cultivate such growth in grace in three ways:

1. Walk in the Spirit. First, we can cultivate spiritual fruit by walking in the Spirit. As we walk in the Spirit, and live our lives under the Spirit's guidance, spiritual fruit are produced and mature in our lives (Gal. 5:16-18; 22-23). Walking in the Spirit includes crucifying the flesh with its passions and desires (Gal. 5:24), setting one's mind on what the Spirit desires (Rom. 8:5), being controlled by the Spirit (Rom. 8: 8), putting to death the works of the flesh (Rom. 8:13), and being led by the Spirit (Rom. 8:14).

2. Abide in Christ. Second, we can cultivate spiritual fruit by abiding in Christ. Jesus taught that as we abide, or remain, in Him, spiritual fruit is produced in our lives (John 15:1-8). He described Himself as the main stem of the vine, and us as the branches. If a branch is severed from the vine, it will die, but if it abides in the vine, it will live and produce fruit. The same is true of us. If we remain in Christ, we will produce fruit. If we detach ourselves, we will die.

3. Means of Grace. Third, we can cultivate spiritual fruit by attending to the means of grace. By "means of grace," we refer to those spiritual disciplines that cause a believer to mature and grow in grace.

They include, among other things, prayer and worship, fellowship with other Christians, and reading and meditating on the Bible.

Both spiritual gifts and spiritual fruit are necessary elements of the Christian life. If we, as God's missionary people, are to fully represent Him to the world, we must exhibit both in abundance. As unbelievers see spiritual gifts in operation in the church, they are brought face to face with Christ's awesome power. As they see the fruit manifested in Christians, they are shown His beautiful character.

Walking with the Holy Spirit

Now that you have concluded today's reading, take a few moments to complete the following exercise.

A Truth to Embrace: If the world is to see Christ in me, I must allow the Spirit to produce His fruit in my life.

A Commitment to Make: I commit myself to cultivate spiritual fruit in my life by daily abiding in Christ and walking in the Spirit.

A Prayer to Pray: Holy Spirit, I yield myself to You that You may produce in me the character of Jesus.

A Verse to Memorize: "But the fruit of the Spirit is love, joy, peace, patience, kindness, goodness, faithfulness, gentleness, and self-control. Against such things there is no law." (Gal. 5:22-23)

Other Works by Denzil R. Miller

Walking with the Apostles: 45 Days in the Book of Acts

Power Ministry: How to Minister in the Spirit's Power
(2004) (Also available in French, Portuguese, Romanian,
Malagasy, Kinyarwanda, and Chichewa)

*Empowered for Global Mission: A Missionary
Look at the Book of Acts* (2005)

From Azusa to Africa to the Nations (2005)
(Also available in French, Spanish, and Portuguese)

*In Step with the Spirit: Studies in the
Spirit-filled Walk* (2008)

*The Kingdom and the Power: The Kingdom of God:
A Pentecostal Interpretation* (2009).
Second edition (2017)

*Experiencing the Spirit: A Study of the Work of
the Spirit in the Life of the Believer* (2009)

Teaching in the Spirit (2009)

*Power Encounter: Ministering in the Power and
Anointing of the Holy Spirit: Revised* (2009)
(Also available in French, Portuguese, Romanian,
Kiswahili and Chichewa)

*You Can Minister in God's Power: A Guide for
Spirit-filled Disciples* (2009)

Proclaiming Pentecost: 100 Sermon Outlines on the Power of the Holy Spirit (2011) Associate editor with Mark Turney, editor (Also available in French, Spanish, Portuguese, Moore, Amharic, Swahili, Chichewa, and Kirundi)

Proclaiming Christ to the Nations: 100 Sermon Outlines on Spirit-Empowered Mission (2107)

Globalizing Pentecostal Missions in Africa (2011) Editor, with Enson Lwesya (Also available in French, 2014)

The Spirit of God in Mission: A Vocational Commentary on the Book of Acts (2013)

The 1:8 Promise of Jesus: The Key to World Harvest (2012)

Power for Mission: The Africa Assemblies of God Mobilizing to Reach the Nations (2014) Editor, with Enson Lwesya

Missionary Tongues Revisited: More than an Evidence: Revisiting Luke's Missional Perspective on Speaking in Tongues (2014)

These and other books can be purchased on the author's website: www.DenzilRMiller.com

CPSIA information can be obtained
at www.ICGtesting.com
Printed in the USA
FFOW05n1928171217

9 780997 175042